PRAISE FOR
THE SOUL-SOURCED ENTREPRENEUR

"If Christine Kane didn't already exist, the world would have to create her. The Soul-Sourced approach to business success, rooted in sound strategy and soul-searching authenticity, is exactly what today's entrepreneurs want and need. What a beautiful, powerful book!"

—JOHN DAVID MANN, coauthor of the
international bestseller *The Go-Giver*

"Do you want to know how entrepreneurship is being redefined? By ditching the winner-take-all tactics and leaning into authenticity and integrity. Christine Kane's book shows you how to achieve the business of your dreams, the right way. Arguably, the only way."

—MIKE MICHALOWICZ, author of
Fix This Next and *Profit First*

"Christine Kane is the best kind of business owner and teacher: the kind that leads with her soul. Money, yes. Success, yes. But soul first. She understands and teaches us that power, our true superpower, doesn't come from being in charge, having money, or always knowing what to do. It comes from tapping into the deepest part of our intuition and intention. She reminds us that it's not the business we create or even what it does that truly matters, but rather who we become in the process. Christine is a refreshing voice of patience in a business world so busy rushing, it often misses the point. I highly recommend this book and all of Christine's work."

—BROOKE CASTILLO, founder of The Life Coach School

"Leader, entrepreneur, and business coach Christine Kane has helped thousands take their business ideas from concept to six or seven figures. She explains how you can do so too, by flipping 'it's business, not personal' on its head. Business is personal, she says, and in fact the more personal you make it, the more impact you will have. If you want to be successful, powerful, and influential but are repulsed by admonishments to crush, hack, manipulate, and succeed through pure 24/7 aggression, this is the book you've been waiting for. In this inspiring and practical guide, Kane points to those qualities you may have deemed problematic—vulnerability, sensitivity, creativity, intuition—as the path to lasting success. She offers practical advice about navigating mindset obstacles, figuring out your relationship to money, and owning your true power. This special book is a missing link for all of us who long to succeed on our own terms. With warmth, humor, and wisdom earned in the trenches, Kane explains that you already have everything you need to build a wildly rewarding and soul-satisfying business."

—SUSAN PIVER, *New York Times* bestselling
author and founder of The Open Heart Project

"Finally, a business guide that celebrates that business is personal and vulnerability is strength. Christine Kane's approach to entrepreneurship deepens our integrity, clarity, and connection to others. Eye-opening, affirming, and downright practical, *Soul-Sourced Entrepreneur* is a must-read for all mindful, vision-driven business owners."

—KRISTINE CARLSON, *New York Times* bestselling
coauthor of the Don't Sweat the Small Stuff series

"In *The Soul-Sourced Entrepreneur*, Christine Kane does the brave work that's behind any business owner's daily reality. She shows readers how to drop the struggle and build their businesses using self-awareness and vulnerability as strategic assets and opportunities, not things to conceal. A true embodiment of authenticity and resilience!"

—HAL ELROD, international keynote speaker and bestselling
author of *The Miracle Morning* and *The Miracle Equation*

the
SOUL
SOURCED
ENTREPRENEUR

the
SOUL
SOURCED
ENTREPRENEUR

An Unconventional Success Plan
for the **HIGHLY CREATIVE**,
SECRETLY SENSITIVE, and
WILDLY AMBITIOUS

CHRISTINE KANE

BenBella Books, Inc.
Dallas, TX

BenBella Books, Inc.
10440 N. Central Expressway, Suite 800
Dallas, TX 75231
www.benbellabooks.com
Send feedback to feedback@benbellabooks.com

BenBella is a federally registered trademark.

Printed in the United States of America
10 9 8 7 6 5 4 3 2 1

Library of Congress Control Number: 2020028127
ISBN 9781950665440 (trade cloth)
ISBN 9781950665563 (electronic)

Editing by Greg Brown
Copyediting by Scott Calamar
Proofreading by Jenny Bridges and Sarah Beck
Text design and composition by Jessika Rieck
Cover design by Jack Kinley
Printed by Lake Book Manufacturing

Distributed to the trade by Two Rivers Distribution, an Ingram brand
www.tworiversdistribution.com

This book goes out to every creative, smart, passionate person who started a cool business and still has those secret days where they wonder if they're really cut out for all of this shit.

CONTENTS

MANAGING POWER

INTERPRETING EXPERIENCES

NAVIGATING DECISIONS

ON BEING "CUT OUT"
FOR BUSINESS (OR WHY
YOU NEED THIS BOOK)

I t was like getting a winning lottery ticket.

I won a contest. The prize was a phone call with a *New York Times* best-selling author who was a coach, guru, and strategist. We're talking Oprah Book Club status. I'd get twenty minutes of coaching on anything. From my hero! A person whose books I'd devoured! Happy day!

At this time—just three years into my career as a songwriter—I'd never talked with a coach. I hardly ever got to talk to anyone about the challenges that came with following my dreams and making a business happen.

I figured I had some good stuff going for me. For starters, I was living my passion. This author was a motivational maven, all about passion and purpose. She'd love that part, right?

But the reality of this "living my passion" stuff was hard. Harder than I'd ever imagined. Writing songs and performing was one thing. Trying to run a business, manage a mailing list, track numbers and money, hire an assistant who didn't show up to my home office stoned—all while learning how to promote myself and my art—was a whole other game. I was in new territory constantly.

So I wanted . . . what? Encouragement? Strategy? Compassion? I didn't know. At the time, I had no clue what to expect or even what best-selling authors did in these sessions.

I dialed in at the appointed hour. The famous author got on the line and informed me—first and foremost—we had a hard stop time. Another winner was up after me, so we had to move quickly. Then she wanted background. She wanted data. She needed numbers. She asked for my income streams. She wanted to know my three-year plan, my five-year plan, and my ten-year plan.

I tripped over my words giving her the basics: I had just released my second CD on my own record label. I'd started to write songs for my third. I was touring all over the country. I had a booking agent.

Then I moved on to my numbers, which were simple and not even sort of impressive. I'd never heard of "income streams," so I skipped that part. And, oops, I didn't have a plan—three, five, ten, or otherwise. I could barely figure out what the next month would look like.

After fifteen minutes of back and forth, the famed author reached her conclusion.

"Look," she said. "I'm sorry. But your situation isn't sustainable. You need to give this up and go get a job. You've discovered something crucial here—business is hard. Especially the entertainment industry."

She went on to tell me it was time to get serious about the rest of my life and "be a good steward of my financial future." Then she apologized for having to be the one to deliver the truth. Her final words went like this: "Some people just aren't cut out for business. Even fewer for the arts. You can be good at other things."

Then she moved on to the next lucky winner.

I have friends who, in this situation, would've hung up the phone and uttered a clear and cosmic "fuck you!" to this author. They would make it their life's mission to prove her wrong. Possibly even waiting until the exact pinnacle of their blinding success to write her a lengthy letter listing the many ways she had failed and concluding, with their final flip-of-the-bird assessment, that she was a fraud. Then they'd post it all on YouTube.

I'm not one of those people.

In fact, this single, meager conversation landed me in a cesspool of self-doubt. I was left wondering what it even meant to be "cut out" for business, for the arts, or for anything involving having an idea and going for it.

Her opinions haunted me, but I ultimately didn't follow the best-selling author's advice. I didn't go get a job. In fact, in the years following that conversation, I went on to release five more CDs and a DVD that won a Telly Award. All of this added up to sell more than 100,000 units—a sizable amount in the indie music arena. I toured with some amazing entertainers and musicians. Two dance companies choreographed ballets to my music, taking me on tour with their troupes.

And here's where it gets weirder.

Along the way, fans with dreams of turning their ideas and side hustles into real businesses would wait until I'd signed CDs after my shows. Then they'd furtively ask for my advice. They wanted me to tell them how I'd done it. How had I built such a solid business while staying true to my art and myself? How had I dealt with hard stuff like rejection and sales and assholes?

I shared everything I could in the time it took to pack up my gear. These informal backstage chats turned into weekend retreats, which turned into mentoring. Eventually, I devoted myself to coaching full-time, starting a business that grew into a multimillion dollar company called Uplevel You.

And, you know what? That best-selling author was 100 percent right.

I wasn't cut out for any of it. At least, not by the rules of conventional business types like her. In fact, she was just one of many "experts" I'd meet on my entrepreneurial path who never considered there might be a different set of rules for extraordinary success. Years after my experience with that author, I hired a consultant. He was a whip-smart strategist, a serial entrepreneur, and, yes, also an author of a best-selling book. This was long after I'd proven myself in music and a few years into coaching and Uplevel You. The consultant spent much of the first morning with my operations director poring over spreadsheets and numbers. After that, he wanted to sit down with me, the owner and founder. Now that he'd seen the metrics, waded through our programs and products, and gotten the background, he wanted to know some things. Namely, my ten-year plan.

"I don't do ten-year plans," I told him. Before he could counter, I inserted, "And I don't do five-year plans either. Next question."

He stared at me. He held up our financial statements. He slapped them with the back of his hand, looking me up and down. "Then here's what I want to know," he said. "How did someone like *you* get so profitable in business?" Then, apparently realizing his question was loaded with judgment, he made a weak attempt to smile at me.

I smiled back. But the words "someone like you" rang in my ears. I'd heard it enough at that point to know what he meant: someone who was not like him or all the other hard-hitting, strategy-driven, left-brained, go-get-'em, break-the-board, walk-over-coals, fake-it-'til-you-make-it, sacrifice-everything-for-the-sale business types. What he meant was someone who used words like "intuition," "instinct," and "soul" a little too freely, while cringing at words like "compete," "dominate," "crush," and "blast." Someone who didn't plow forward on a linear path focused on a single and self-serving endpoint. And someone who used a clear (and, perhaps, odd) set of internal measures to guide next steps every bit as much as the usual external measures of money and numbers.

What he meant was how could someone like me or the thousands of clients Uplevel You attracts become so wildly successful in their businesses?

The answer to his question is what this book and my life's work are all about.

If you've read this far, chances are you're no stranger to the struggles of starting or having your own business.

It looks like this:

You try. Hey, you're not lazy. You really want this to work. You've watched all the right TED Talks, done all the best launch programs, copywriting programs, selling-from-the-stage programs. Sure, they've shown you a few things, but you always end up face-to-face with the same old issues and setbacks.

So, you settle.

There's an endless list of things you tolerate, whether they're the same meager annual income, or that one client who makes you want to hurl yourself off a cliff each week, or the stress of trying to make it all work on your own. All while wishing there was a way to raise the bar to a level you know you deserve.

And you wonder.

If you're *really* cut out for this. If your siblings or well-meaning friends were right all along when they said you weren't aggressive enough, organized enough, clear enough, or data-driven enough. You wonder if you're too tender on the inside and too scattered on the outside. Or maybe even if you might just have the ever-ubiquitous, pseudo-spiritual diagnosis of "bad energy."

So, your question remains: Is it possible to have a wildly profitable and successful business without adopting character traits that are false, phony, manipulative, or robotically corporate? Can you succeed while still being you?

The answer is a resounding yes.

There's a new class of business owner on the rise. I call them Soul-Sourced Entrepreneurs. They understand a key distinction most people miss: It's not just about *having* the six-figure business. It's about *becoming* the person who can create and own a six- or even seven-figure business. They want the indescribable feeling of confidence that comes when you cross the six-figure line *your way* while knowing you have the power to do it again and again. They want to employ their own reliable, unique set of best practices, based as much on intuition and self-awareness as on specific skills and strategies. Most important, they want to trust their choices and actions every day, unfettered by the gnawing feeling of self-doubt.

In other words, the *what* is no longer enough. The Soul-Sourced Entrepreneur wants the *how*. Namely, how to navigate and grow a business sourced from a solid and serene place that isn't about the usual round of old-school rules and behaviors, which are little more than a sad and dusty collection of memorized illusions at this point.

That's exactly how I, and thousands of my clients, did it. And I'm going to teach you everything I know.

How is this book different?

Well, for one thing, I'm not going to tell you to change your style, your instincts, your sensitivity level, or your emotions. I'm going to assume you've already read stacks of books on business and mindset and have exhausted yourself trying to follow behavioral prescriptions that didn't work.

Second, this is not a "law-of-attraction" manual where I tell you to be more positive so you can get more goodies. Frankly, the waters of having a business are often murky and rough. The stakes are high, and pressure is everywhere. Adding the mandate of perpetual positivity is ludicrous and often disastrous. I happen to know you're fine, even with your doubts, even with your anxieties, and all the other shit you secretly judge yourself for doing or not doing, being or not being, or not measuring up to.

Third, this book is not a magic pill. Despite what all the cool internet marketer kids say, there's no one-size-fits-all email template that's going to fill your shopping cart with bags of money while you're out surfing or getting laid.

What we'll do together, however, is better than that.

We will build a source of unfathomable strength by following a simple framework that grants you access to a deep level of internal power.

When my clients sign up for our Uplevel masterminds, they're required to check a box that says, "I'm In." It's a commitment and a promise to others in the group, to their coaches, and to themselves. As an acronym, "I'M IN" also holds the framework of this book. It's the process for becoming a Soul-Sourced Entrepreneur and gaining the keys to mastering your business, your energy, and your dreams.

I: **Initiating Intention** tosses out the old-school, goal-setting models and shows you how to use your life as the force that shapes your intentions. It replaces outward, aggressive, grabby goals with an internal model for intention, based in wisdom and clarity. Here, you'll uncover the traps that keep you confused and overwhelmed, while tuning in to a level of purpose and direction you've never before explored.

M: **Managing Power** is a call to examine your own behavioral patterns for clues to what's been holding you back. Here, you learn to amplify your awareness and clean up the spaces and distractions draining your energy and power.

I: **Interpreting Experiences** is a deep dive into the higher meaning only you can bring to the circumstances arising in your business.

Many entrepreneurs live by default, running into the same walls and telling the same emotionally charged stories. Here's where you ditch that cycle and discover how to find the opportunities hidden within the challenges, while training yourself to access a Soul-Sourced level of strength.

N: Navigating Decisions is where we jettison the word "should" once and for all and break free from fear-based decision-making. We also test the most insidious assumptions and thought patterns that corrupt our otherwise powerful intuitive processes. You'll learn to make intention-based decisions that free you from the fears and confines of past mistakes so you can lead your business with profound clarity.

Some will dismiss what I teach as too "woo," too soft, or maybe even too simplistic. I expect that. But consider that year after year of listening to the admonishments of those old-school business drones has likely left you mistrusting yourself, the world, and your own power. That's a horrible place to spend your time.

Instead, hang out with me for a bit and tune into an intuitive, Soul-Sourced business that gives you the permission you've been waiting for to release the manipulative, inauthentic, and just plain hard things you've lugged around for far too long. You're about to enter a world that's more powerful than "five easy steps" and more motivating than boring "best practices." It's a world you're cut out for, my friend. More importantly, it's cut out for you, your soul, and the dreamlike levels of success you know are possible.

STRATEGY & SOUL

1

THE GREED INDUSTRY

Grove Park Inn, Asheville, North Carolina, 2:15 PM

J ohn was built like a fighter. He was solid and thin, with hard edges.
"You're Christine," he said, looking down at me before I could
get out of the hotel lobby chair. Even though I was the one inter-
viewing him for a job in my company, John had already established himself
squarely in the alpha role. After a firm handshake, we began.

The conversation was interesting enough. He certainly had the chops.
He'd worked for just about every big-name guru, leader, and player in the
coaching industry, and he shared stories of legal battles, road tours, and
billions of dollars generated seemingly overnight.

I, on the other hand, had a tiny coaching company. I'd crossed the
million-dollar mark, but my team was all virtual. To someone like John,
my business was barely out of diapers. I had just purchased a 3,500-square-
foot office space downtown and was hiring my first full-time operations
director. I admitted that the position was well below his pay grade.

"I know that," he said casually. "I'm only here because I saw your ad and
wanted to see who in this town could possibly be in the greed industry."

I stopped. "The *what* industry?" (I thought he'd said "green.")

"The greed industry," he repeated. "It's what we're all in. Real estate investment. Financial advising. Self-help. It doesn't matter. It's about making money. That's why we do what we do. Plain and simple."

He paused to snap his gum.

"But you," he pointed at me as if I were exhibit B, "I can tell by looking at you that you're clearly *not* in the greed industry. You think you can change people. You're doing the whole 'transformation' thing." He said the word "transformation" like it was a turd that had found its way into his mouth.

"Which means what?" I asked.

"Which means you believe people change. You believe you're out to do good in the world—you know, like I said, 'transformation.'"

"Hold on a minute." I pointed at one of the names listed on his work history. "*He* believes in transformation."

"No, he doesn't! He's the greed industry, too," John laughed. "Listen, you better get very clear about one thing: You got a business here. You wanna be in the real world and make money? Or are you going to float along in la-la land believing you're all about helping people? Because that's your choice."

This interview had taken an unexpected turn. I didn't answer. Instead, I looked down at my list of scripted interview questions, desperately scanning for one that would change the subject and get this thing back in my control.

"So," I said, "tell me three things you're really great at."

John stared at me. Then he sighed and answered the question. The conversation lagged on for a bit and closed coolly. When he finally stood up and walked away, I took a deep breath.

"Well, that went well, don't you think?" I said aloud to no one.

In my fantasies, after John walked away, I didn't give him another thought. In my fantasies, I said, "Next!" with the appropriate degree of coldness in my voice and shook the hand of the next candidate in line for the job.

The truth was, John was my only interview that day. After he left, a voice began gnawing its way through my head. *What if he's right? What if I'm too soft and sensitive and fluffy?* This wasn't the first time I'd faced doubts like these. When I was a musician, building my own record label and meeting industry executives along the way, I'd gotten glimpses of the colder side of the entertainment business, the part kept behind closed doors and run by people just like John. Their eyes always seemed to say, "You will not survive me. Don't even try."

My encounter with John unearthed the same old internal questions I'd faced in those years, and they stayed with me for days after.

Was there, in fact, some "real world" of business, where the big boys with their massive left brains crush each other with a competitive, elbows-out, my-will-against-yours approach?

Did that mean success was really all about greed and aggression?

Was my business less real and less likely to succeed if I didn't play that game?

Was I, in fact, as John implied, a clueless idealist, off in la-la land?

And, if I wasn't, then what separated people like me from the Johns of the world? What was the difference?

Over the coming days, I slowly came back to center. The crazy, shame-y voices of panic and doom started to dissipate. The wise part of me—neither cold nor aggressive in its clarity—revealed the answers I was looking for.

And you know what? The answers had nothing to do with greed. Or transformation.

The difference between my approach to business and John's was all in how we view the world and how we see ourselves in relation to the world. It has a lot to do with trust. And with control.

A world that can't be trusted is a world that must be controlled. The Johns of the world crave control because they live by an old, worn-out set of rules. They don't trust themselves, their intuition, other people, or the paths of their souls (a word that, of course, makes them cringe). So, they steadfastly follow "the Old Rules." They're relegated to the use of force, will, manipulation, and seemingly flawless logic to create the results they most want. And the results they most want are all about the numbers.

Naturally, business owners like you and me look like pansies. We follow a new set of rules—let's call them "the Soul Rules"—and we're pioneering our way into a new approach to business. An approach that allows for trust in the world and in ourselves. To those who follow "the Old Rules," you and I seem lost in some airy-fairy land of energy and spirituality. We don't have a clue how business really works.

I call bullshit. Take a moment to consider the differences in the worldviews of these two different styles of business.

Old Rule: Don't go into business to compete. Go into business to dominate.

Soul Rule: Domination is a fixed position. If and when you arrive there, you spend the best part of your life defending that position. (Remember the last time you reached your "goal weight"? What then?) Don't kid yourself: this is a miserable place. Focus instead on the energy of what you do. And be flexible and fluid. Get comfortable with transition. Don't be trapped by the ego's demand for fixed positions and the illusion of arrival.

Old Rule: Do what it takes, no matter what that is.

Soul Rule: Work hard, sure. But align with the truth of yourself. Money is not your only driver. If something feels wrong, it probably is. Your energy is always speaking to you.

Old Rule: Don't just double your business, 10× your business. Better yet, 20× your business. Scale everything.

Soul Rule: More doesn't always equal more freedom. If more money comes with more stress, more pressure, more complexity, and less quality—then it's not worth it. Scaling is not the right path for every business. And not the right path at every moment. Know yourself before you blindly grab for more.

Old Rule: There are rules of business, and you follow them. That's the fastest way to success.

Soul Rule: When you follow rules and standards just to follow rules and standards, you end up trapped in the land of the left brain. Subsequently, you miss out on the true wisdom you're being called to bring to your business. You can only experience that wisdom by stepping away from the mental noise and discovering deeper places of insight.

Old Rule: Make a strategy (a three-year plan, or, better yet, a ten-year plan!) and relentlessly stick to it.

Soul Rule: Initiate intention and practice it. Create a strategy and be flexible and present enough to make changes when they're needed. (And they will always be needed.)

Old Rule: Business is business is business.

Soul Rule: Your business is the playing field for your soul's expansion. Any time you clear an internal obstacle that arises, you uplevel to a new phase of your growth.

What you'll find behind the Soul Rules is not a group of entrepreneurs lost in some airy-fairy land with no clue how business works. You'll find a new breed of entrepreneurs playing by a new set of highly effective rules. Rules that fit their beliefs and values. You'll find the Soul-Sourced Entrepreneurs.

So, who are these Soul-Sourced Entrepreneurs?

The psychotherapist who breaks the conventions of her industry and works *only* with her specific, ideal client (not whoever walks through the door)—thereby freeing up both the emotional energy and the time to create a popular online group program and later write what becomes a best-selling book.

The real estate agent who knows the houses she helps clients buy and sell are elements of their whole beings and builds her business around this truth.

The metalsmith who honors the stories behind the custom jewelry she creates, knowing her pieces carry energy and are more than just bling.

The hospital employee who sees a need for an association and *starts* one, ditching the old medical model in favor of something that truly calls its tribe to elevate.

The corporate sales director who realizes she has a bigger calling than a corner office in a dysfunctional work environment and quits to build an empire. Her mission? To transform the corporate workplace.

You'll meet people like this and many others throughout this book. The options are limitless, really. Results will vary because this path is based in strategy *and* soul, something deeper than the confines of current business models. We begin at the beginning by dismantling the old, rigid structure that forced you out of your authentic entrepreneurial self. Then we create a new paradigm for you and your business.

2

TRADING TRICKS FOR TRACKS

G ot it," Tracey said.

Then, more silence on the other end of the phone. "Still taking a few notes here. Gimme a sec."

Another pause. "Okay. Done!" she said proudly.

Tracey was a new client. She and I were mapping out her next launch, a three-month mentoring program for amateur photographers. We walked through the email sequences. I edited her copy and made some changes to her landing pages. We laid out a plan.

We were about to hang up when Tracey sighed, "Well, let's see if I can go pull this off."

Alarms sounded in my head. *"Pull this off"*? Really? Did she think this was trickery?

Let's see if I can convince people I'm better than I really am.

Let's see if I can force people to do something I don't believe they should do.

Let's see if I can get by for another day in my business.

I made Tracey stay on the phone with me well past her coaching time so we could dig into this decidedly small mindset.

Like many entrepreneurs, Tracey had created a business by accident. She was a successful artist and designer. Then she got invitations to teach. Then she created workshops. After that, she started offering those same programs online.

Truth was, the word "business" felt foreign to her, and she never really saw herself as the owner of one. In her words, "I'm an artist. I kinda just wing it when it comes to marketing and other business stuff." And yes, selling always felt like trickery. Like she was getting away with something.

"Underneath?" she confessed. "This whole thing feels like a sham."

Tracey is not alone. This is a common sentiment.

You may work miracles with your designs, your coaching, or your healing. But when it comes to your business itself, that sense of confidence is gone. Your business feels heavy. And you feel incompetent. So, you avoid the business side of your business.

Until you can't.

Then you force yourself to make that sales call, post something lame on social media, or rush through a tax statement, secretly feeling like a five-year-old putting on your mom's heels and lipstick, clomping around the house pretending to be an adult. You feel like a fraud—or like Tracey, as if you're "pulling something off," rather than creating it from a place of truth.

Tracey admitted that a "smoke and mirrors Tracey" would take over in most situations involving her business. This was a Tracey she was supposed to be, not the real person.

"Which is probably why I'm always anxiety-ridden," she said. "I don't know exactly who's running this thing."

Tracey's uncertainty and confusion led her to trust other people more than herself. Some guy on a webinar tells you that "this thing" works. So, you're off and running, trying "this thing." Maybe it works. If it doesn't, you try the next "this thing."

The problem these days is that the internet is a never-ending stream of "this thing." You can easily get hooked into believing your business is about finding "the thing" that will pull it off and make all your business troubles vanish.

In the long run, it fails.

Tactics are just dress up. They won't work in the real world any more than that five-year-old girl can put on her mother's shoes, saunter into a liquor store, and buy a bottle of Hendrick's. What the Soul-Sourced Entrepreneur is seeking has nothing to do with dress up. She wants confidence. An ability to self-direct and self-correct. She wants to be unflappable, unstoppable, and clear.

I told Tracey that the clarity and confidence she wanted were there for the taking. You get them by walking—consciously and simultaneously—on two tracks in your business: the Strategy Track and the Soul Track.

THE TWO TRACKS

The first track, the Strategy Track, is the left-brain stuff that everyone equates with business success: marketing, sales, systems, sequences, operations. When you read most business books, this is the track they're laying down: How to close a room. How to create an A-level team. How to scale your company. How to spreadsheet everything from your profits, your losses, your daily life, your productivity, your morning poops . . . you name it.

While you do need to understand these things to operate a successful business, the second track, the Soul Track, is where the rubber meets the road. And that's what this book focuses on.

The Soul Track is the soft stuff. The stuff that's dismissed as woo-woo. It's the energy behind the Strategy Track. It's what makes your business authentic. Think of strategy as a cupcake tin. It's the necessary equipment that provides the structure. Soul, then, is all the ingredients that go into that cupcake tin. Your unique recipe. And that recipe—not the tin—determines what your cupcake (your business) will be. When you focus on those ingredients—like who exactly your client is, who you are, what your core message is, and how you serve the clients—people know it. They know you've made a stellar fucking cupcake. You know it, too. And your business grows from that genuine place.

The Soul Track is also where your obstacles like to hang out, smoking and drawing graffiti all over the walls. When you're unconsciously vandalizing your success—not charging enough money, doing work that bores you, or keeping abusive clients—your business is most likely calling you to check out what's going on in the Soul Track.

As you master this mindset or "soul" stuff, you naturally become expert at identifying, selecting, and executing tactics (the "strategy" stuff) that produce the kind of business you want.

Not everyone is excited to take this on. In the end, Tracey wasn't. She loved the *idea* of the Soul Track. But during our months working together, she kept coming to our calls with more tactics to help her avoid the deeper work the Soul Track demands. The longer she avoided her own expansion, the more tactics she kept coming up with. I realized she'd rather play the dreaded smoke-and-mirrors game than experience true confidence.

Ultimately, I let Tracey go as a client.

In truth, the Soul Track isn't easy. We live in a culture that dedicates billions of dollars—whether through games, movies, apps, pills, pings, or porn—in an effort to distract from or avoid anything that's the least bit uncomfortable or uncertain. We've become well trained to find a quick fix.

With that in mind, business owners who dare to simultaneously navigate these two tracks are a rare breed. They relentlessly tune in at a level most people can't even conceive. They're a hybrid of entrepreneur and alchemist, jettisoning the old rules of business and using their personal energy as a compass in uncharted territory. But their ranks are not closed. In fact, there's a place for you among them as well. It's just a matter of finding your way in authentically.

3

THE NEW OPS MANUAL: EIGHT GUIDELINES FOR THE SOUL TRACK

When I was an up-and-coming musician, I got offered a record deal. Every piece and part of my ego examined this prospect and binged on it. Oh, how I loved the idea of a stage introduction that went, "Ladies and gentlemen, please welcome [insert impressive sounding record label] recording artist Christine Kane." I loved the built-in credibility: *"Ha! This proves it! I'm legit."* I also loved that important people were paying attention to me.

But there was a problem. While much of me grabbed and clutched at the idea of a record deal, this small, persistent presence deep within sensed that this was the wrong thing for my creative growth and for this business I was building. The money the record label was offering wouldn't sustain me at a time when two-thirds of my revenue came from directly selling my CDs. The creative freedom to make my CDs the way I wanted would most certainly vanish. And I had this creepy sense that the A&R guy saw me mostly as the next shiny object in his collection, while offering me the standard, underhanded deal.

Plus, there was the deeper issue of me not believing I was legit on my own. What the hell was that all about? At the time, my little indie record label was doing really, really well. No, I didn't have the contacts a major label would give me—but I didn't have the restrictions either. I was successful by anyone's standards, and wildly successful for an independent musician and songwriter. Why wasn't that enough for me? Why did I need someone else's label to prove my worth? Why was I still trying to get discovered?

In the end, as hard as it was, I ultimately wrestled the decision from the sticky hands of my ego and turned down the deal.

It was a Soul Track decision—though I didn't call it that at the time. Back then, there were no guidelines to turn to as I stepped away from the conventional path, making an authentic choice for myself and my business.

Over the years, as I've helped clients create their own unconventional success stories, I've shared several guiding principles that can help one adhere to the Soul Track, even when the shiniest objects try to tempt us away. Think of these eight guidelines as the New Soul-Sourced Ops Manual. Keep them in mind as you read this book. With their guidance, you can transform your business and yourself.

GUIDELINE #1: YOUR BUSINESS IS THE PLAYING FIELD FOR YOUR SOUL'S EXPANSION

Let's face it. No matter what all the hyped-up internet marketers tell you about all the millions you'll make, all the caviar you'll eat, all the waves you'll surf, and all the sex you'll have as the money rolls in, business is hard.

That's because when you commit to building a business, you commit to generating your own (and other people's) income. You commit to managing your own spirit, your own time, and your own relationships. When you do this, there's no handing over your responsibility to "the man." There's no convenient person out there to blame. You now own all of it. There's no half-assing anything anymore. Everything is whole-assed.

Subsequently, your business will deliver all the private revelations you need for evolving your soul. Got fears about being seen? You get to heal those and loosen the tight grip of the image-obsessed ego. Get floored by shame every time you raise your prices? Cleaning up these emotional patterns is the next step. In other words, your business will force you to be aware of and remain in relationships with money, people, communication, ego, challenges, fear, and time—all of which will deliver the real breakthroughs that carry you to your next level of expansion.

GUIDELINE #2: SOFT IS HARD

"Soft is hard" is a favorite expression of Tom Peters, business strategist and best-selling coauthor of *In Search of Excellence*. In interviews, Peters says, "I'm an engineer. I believe in numbers. I believe in measurement—but then there's the other ninety-five percent, which is the human part."

As the business owner, you are the human part.

Everyone thinks they want more strategy. "Just tell me what to do," says a typical coaching client. And by "what to do," they usually mean some tidy left-brain, numbers-based fix that will skyrocket their email-open rate, make customers swarm, and place them squarely at the top of their industry.

Sadly, only a handful of these people are willing to go soft and address the energy behind the strategy. The ones who do go there usually end up with the hard results they want—hard results that are in alignment with the soul of their business.

GUIDELINE #3: COMMITMENT CREATES CONFIDENCE (NOT THE OTHER WAY AROUND)

Many people wait for confidence to show up before they commit to an idea or a new direction. But think of anything that's worthwhile in your life—the book you wrote, the product you launched, the children you had, the business you created. Nothing worthwhile in your life happened because you had the confidence first. It happened because you committed to making it happen. The confidence showed up as you courageously took steps forward.

GUIDELINE #4: BECOMING IS THE NEW GETTING

When you set an intention, you are here: *Point A*.

The thing you want is out there: *Point B*.

So, what's next? Well, with the old-school model, we sprint as fast as possible, with all our determination and might, to seize Point B. We achieve things. We grab things. We wrestle things to the ground.

And, of course, we *get* things. We get clients. We get money. We get lean, get fit, get high, get down, get up, get drunk, get rich, or get laid. Get 'er done. We're a culture of getters.

Point B? Mine. Gimme.

The truth? The energy of getting is sad. It's isolating. It leaves you wired up and wiry. Plus, grabbing and getting make you miss out on the best part of all: who you *become* on the way to Point B. All the stuff *between* Point A and Point B. In this middle ground, you become someone who does more than *reach* Point B or *gets* to Point B. You become someone who *merges* with Point B. You become someone who can *own* Point B.

GUIDELINE #5: CURIOSITY IS THE NEW CERTAINTY

If I had a nickel for every sure decision I've made since I became an entrepreneur, I'd have zero nickels.

I've made decisions to launch programs that ultimately made millions, despite people on my own team predicting their failure.

I've chosen to fire people who were perfectly lovely human beings but weren't a match for my work style or our company culture.

I've decided to hold my events in Asheville (my home) instead of a major city, when more than a few strategists told me I was making a huge mistake.

If you talk to most entrepreneurs behind closed doors, you discover that while they like to toss around phrases like "due diligence," more often than not, the real driver of their business decisions falls closer to the phrase "pull it out your ass."

Certainty, they'll tell you, is an illusion.

If you're the owner, the entrepreneur, the creative, the one with the ideas and the vision, then craving certainty will destroy you and your business. Whether you're about to outline your next training or hire your first marketing manager or even just sit down to meditate, the need for certainty—to know how this will turn out—will stifle your creativity and energy.

Curiosity, on the other hand, is freedom. It tells the mind to take a back seat to wonder. Tuned in and open to discovery, our curiosity probes the possibilities with questions, not judgment. *What if? What's next? How would I do that? And then what?* There's no failure, only another inquiry, another thing to try, to learn, to know. Another step in our expansion, in our becoming.

When we approach challenges from a place of curiosity, barriers come down, and we and our businesses enter a stream of positive, forward-moving energy, which is where entrepreneurs need to be.

GUIDELINE #6: MONEY IS ONLY ONE MEASURE IN YOUR BUSINESS

Early on, I discovered through various work-style and strengths-based tests that I am not only *not* wired to manage a business, but the only thing I can claim to be good at is having ideas.

I had to get over my shame and simply accept this fact. After that, I built a team that was a little larger than standard business practices would condone. This meant I had to defend my choices when accountants and other spreadsheet overlords questioned me. For instance, I have both an executive assistant and a personal assistant. Yes, I could opt for higher profits by having fewer people on my team and doing more myself, but I value freedom, and my sanity, over numbers.

Don't get me wrong. I'm not stupid about it. Profit-and-loss statements may make my eyes glaze over, but, as a business owner, I've taken the time to know where the lines are and how to operate at a profit.

But I've also taken the time to know myself. And I pay people who love to do the work that drains me. It's good business for me and my company.

If you're not aware of yourself enough to define your own measures of success, you'll get sucked in by old-school expectations and shame yourself for not "trying harder" or being more like [insert famous cover-girl entrepreneur/author here]. Being a smart Soul-Sourced Entrepreneur means knowing where the standard lines in business are, and then gauging which to cross and knowing why you're crossing them. It means developing a relationship with numbers, money, and other measurables so they work for you—not the other way around.

GUIDELINE #7: AND THIS DOESN'T JUST APPLY TO MONEY—IT ALSO APPLIES TO PEOPLE AND MARKETING

Let's say that in the process of running a marketing campaign, you notice that more people open your emails when you use subject lines that are highly charged and perhaps even questionable to you. The old-school experts say, "Do what works. The numbers never lie! These subject lines get opened!"

But then, over time, you have to try harder and harder, and get noisier and noisier to maintain the same open rate. You're expending all this effort and ignoring your intuition because hey, the numbers never lie.

But what the numbers don't and can't tell you (and what you sense) is that you're whittling away your readers' trust with each of these subject lines. Your subject lines and the emails they introduce need to do more than get clicked on. They must build relationships with those who could be ideal clients and, just as important, release those who aren't. Sure, that means a less impressive open rate, but good marketing is not measured in total clicks but in getting the right people to engage with you.

It takes a strong spirit to pull the plug when convention is cheering you on. It takes clarity to see that numbers can lie when we get addicted to the data they reveal and don't look deeper at the trends they're creating. Soul-Sourced Entrepreneurs come to trust in their own sense of clarity and in their own solutions.

GUIDELINE #8: POWER TO, NOT POWER OVER

A friend of mine—a successful actor, screenwriter, and producer—moved out of Los Angeles to a small hippie town where no one knew him. He was eating barbecue with a group of people one evening and a woman in tie-dye and dreadlocks asked him what he did. He told her. She said, "Oh cool." Then she dug into her coleslaw.

At first, his ego didn't know what to do. *'Oh cool?' That's all? That's all?? You're not impressed?*

But when he sat with it later that night, he had an ah-ha moment. Virtually every conversation he'd ever had in LA was about power—either proving he had the power or finding out who had the power and figuring out how to get some of it. He confessed, "I didn't even realize you could have a conversation just to have a conversation!" He didn't know what to do with people who weren't trying to one-up him or get things from him.

Most of us associate power with dominance. Power over others. Power over circumstances. And, as the hippie chick who clearly had a sense of her own power helped my friend discover, that way of relating to power is tiring and so boring after a while that it gets predictable.

Power—when taken for the subtle energy it is and channeled in a way that's creative and works with your personal system—is so earth-shatteringly simple and so much fun that it's *not* tiring. This kind of power is "power to." Meaning "power to" manifest whatever you envision for yourself, for your business, for the world. That's much more powerful than merely dominating. And it's not only worth spending a lifetime mastering, it's worth having a business just so you *can* master it.

Right now, there's no need to worry about committing this new ops manual to memory. The wisdom, structure, and reassurance of its guidelines will appear repeatedly throughout this book as you move through each phase of the Soul-Sourced process—Initiating Intention, Managing Power, Interpreting Experiences, and Navigating Decisions. You'll find these principles present in everything you do as a Soul-Sourced Entrepreneur. Until, over time, these eight little jewels simply become the way you function.

"BLESS THE BABIES": FOUR YEARS FROM INTENTION TO EMPIRE

Marriott Hotel Ballroom, Dallas, Texas, 8:52 AM

Sue closed her eyes and took a deep breath. It was cold backstage, and being nervous was making her shiver uncontrollably. She could hear murmuring voices and occasional outbursts of laughter from the hundreds who were getting settled in the auditorium for day one of the annual conference. She reminded herself, "These are my peeps. We sold this event out in a matter of days. I don't have to be nervous." But she still was.

Her program director peeked behind the curtains. "We're starting in ten minutes, okay? You good?" Sue nodded. Her heart pounded at the warning. Chrysty grabbed her hand and said, "You're gonna be amazing!" before she slipped back out.

For a fleeting moment, Sue longed for "the old days" when she was a neonatal therapist with predictable shifts at the hospital. Sure, there were days filled with anxiety (it was the NICU, right?)—but she certainly never had to face being the keynote speaker at her own national convention.

She was playing on a bigger stage now, literally. It was right there in front of her, complete with racks of colorful spotlights and the giant backdrop she helped design with her company's logo on it. Then, she smiled with pride. She'd come a long way. And this was exactly what she'd set out to do. How many years ago? Four? Only four? Wow.

Sue had built a movement. All from one single thought she had while on the job, feeling isolated, and fighting yet another losing battle with hospital politics: "Someone needs to start an association for neonatal therapists."

Which is exactly what she did. The association she founded now had more than five hundred members, a handful of sponsorships from some of the most respected medical companies in the world, and she was on her third sold-out conference. Her husband Rob—who had always been the entrepreneur in the family—jokingly called himself "a kept man" now that his wife was so frequently in the public spotlight.

It all began with intention. Intention beat out even the most hardcore battles she faced. She remembered all the times she'd thought to herself, *Shouldn't someone stop me? I mean, shouldn't someone come down from some medical authority on high and give me permission? Or demand certification? Or at least a CEU?*

In other words, in a world where you don't do anything without certification, accreditation, or documentation, how could she possibly move forward with this passion-driven idea? She did what all good entrepreneurs do. She gave *herself* permission. Not easy, but so simple.

Chrysty reappeared. "Okay, you ready?"

Sue took a deep breath and said, "I am."

"Rock this!" Chrysty said. Sue smiled. "I plan to."

Just then, a voice boomed over the speakers: "Ladies and gentlemen, please welcome to the stage the president and founder of the National Association of Neonatal Therapists—Sue Ludwig..."

Sue could hear booming applause, along with shouts and whistles. She took another deep breath. With her eyes closed, she reminded herself that this next hour was all about the people out there whose lives and work she was helping to transform—and, of course, the babies. Bless all those precious babies struggling to survive.

Then Sue told herself what she always told herself when the stakes were high: "Just love this. That's all."

She stepped onto the stage beaming.

INITIATING INTENTION

4

FIREWALKS AND FAST FOOD: TOSSING OUT OLD-SCHOOL GOAL SETTING

After college graduation, my boyfriend and I each headed to different cities.

Kevin went to Wall Street. He was one of a handful of college grads swept up by Merrill Lynch and tossed onto their fast track for success, impressing everyone in his wake.

I, on the other hand, went back to the suburbs of Washington, DC, to live in my parents' house. I got a job at a PR firm called Ogilvy & Mather. I was an administrative assistant. And a bad one at that. My commute was a part-time job in itself, robbing me of twelve hours a week.

In his first month at Merrill Lynch, Kevin got sent to a weeklong productivity training. After that, he was all kinds of fired up. All he wanted to talk about was targets and plans and timelines. He was setting goals and mapping them out. He color coded his to-dos. He charted them into a calendar, using an elaborate system of checks and Xs to move the tasks into new squares on the next day's pages.

I panicked. Goals? I had none. Not that I could think of. I knew only one thing at that time. It was the one thing I knew more clearly than anything else: I hated my job. In fact, I hated *having* a job.

I was riddled with guilt on the phone each night as Kevin described hopping out of bed in the morning, driven by those goals, excited for his commute from Jersey to Manhattan. Not me. In fact, no one else I knew was hopping out of bed, excited about their color-coded days. No one even seemed to *have* goals.

Furthermore, they all seemed okay with this lifestyle of plodding along. When I asked my parents and their friends about it, they said things like, "This is just how it is, Christine. You get used to it. Just be thankful you have a good job."

I tried to imagine myself getting used to it.

No dice.

So, I tried my best to think up a few goals.

Get promoted? Lose ten pounds? Marry Kevin, forget all about goals, and set my sights on being a ninja housewife? (This last one was looking like the most probable scenario.)

About that time, a friend gave me a New Age book about a different kind of goal setting. The premise was that you could change your circumstances by visualizing your dreams. In the book, there was an exercise where you imagine placing your desires into a pink balloon. Then, in your mind's eye, you send that balloon up into the sky, through the clouds, and into the heavens. Repeat this daily and your dreams would manifest.

I tried it on my Metro ride each morning. I stuffed freedom, income, and a better job into that balloon. But every time it began its tenuous ascent, it fell back to the ground with a thud, as if to say, "Nice try, kid. You're not going anywhere." I'd look around on the Metro car and see the dull faces of others whose pink balloons had apparently followed the same trajectory.

That's when I got really scared. I didn't have goals. I couldn't visualize. I didn't know how to keep up with this world of getting what you want. My terror of staying stuck in a job I hated, of never knowing myself, of saying "this is just how it is" to my kids one day was palpable.

Then, one night without knowing it, I stumbled upon "intention."

After a crushing day at work (my boss had berated me yet again for my poor filing skills and lack of organization, big surprise), I sat down to write in my journal. In despair, I opened it up to the next blank page.

And something stopped me.

Instead of hitting the page with my usual complaints and drama, I found myself pausing. I then wrote two words at the top of the page:

"Dear God . . . "

What I proceeded to write was a letter. It opened with a confession. I shared that while I was dutifully grateful for my job, I hated it. I said I didn't know what was wrong with me, and that possibly, I wasn't wired to be employed. I apologized for being how I was and for all of my shortcomings.

With trepidation, I confessed a deeply buried dream I'd shared with exactly no one: to make a living on my own terms as a songwriter.

Mind you, up until that time, my only experience of singing on stage was at a sixth-grade piano recital, where I chickened out after singing the first line of "Scarlet Ribbons," resulting in awkward applause as I painfully took my bow to a confused auditorium. Also, the most I could crank out on a guitar was "Michael Row the Boat Ashore" and a few other songs from the Catholic folk mass. But I loved music and writing more than anything.

Something happened as I wrote those words in my journal. A switch got tripped. Some spark was lit. It felt great to simply be honest, to acknowledge what I wanted—even if I was only sending it out into the void. It was as if some quiet presence out there caught my dream without judgment. And it woke something up in me. This ritual became a nightly session. Each evening, I'd open my page, scribble "Dear God," and let fly.

No color coding. No checks. No Xs. No balloons, pink or otherwise.

This is not where I tell you of the divine directives I received or describe the beams of light that flooded my room. I never got an answer. My hand was never taken over by an ethereal being, dictating instructions to my pleas. I got no response. Zero. Zip.

What I did get was clear on my intention. I stripped myself clean of the clutter of *shoulds* that had, until that point, plagued me. I stopped berating myself for my lackluster attitude toward the workforce, and I let myself want what I wanted. In the process, I aligned with that vision. Something in me began to shift—ever so slightly, ever so imperfectly—each and every day.

How do I know this?

Well, at first, it was just a feeling of utter relief. I was finally letting myself see me clearly. My days felt the slightest bit lighter.

Within a year, I'd left my job. And my boyfriend. I moved and was living rent-free in a small town, which gave me the chance to play guitar, write songs, study music, and slowly prepare myself for the dream I was about to make real. Most of the time, I was terrified. But I was also totally exhilarated, lit up with purpose, like the way I used to be when I was a kid.

That's when things really got interesting. A few years into my music odyssey, and after another move—this time to the city that would become my home, Asheville, North Carolina—I was waiting tables and playing at open mic nights. A friend of mine, also a musician, had to cancel a week-end stint at a local tavern, and he told the owner about me. I got my very first two-night paid gig. A music promoter vacationing in my town was in the audience that weekend—and she booked me for a show in another city. I kept booking more and more dates. Within months, I quit my waitressing job. A year later, I made my first CD in a friend's basement.

In other words, out of a single intention I unknowingly initiated, I began a music career that would lead me to:

- Start my own record label
- Create a home-based office and later move to an outside office space
- Work with agents and managers and then hire my own on-site team
- Write hundreds of songs
- Make and release seven CDs and a DVD
- Start a weekend retreat series in my town that sold out multiple times each year
- Perform thousands of dates around the world
- Found my coaching company, Uplevel You—and write this book

Whether applied to our dreams, businesses, next steps, or simply our days, intention is a powerful force field. When someone initiates intention, they are clarifying the structures of their life or business, harnessing their creative energy, and then responding to the results it draws. This process is doable and replicable, and it begins with tossing out some of the overused and often ineffective approaches to intention. It ends with accessing your authentic, visionary direction.

INTENTION ISN'T A RIGHT ANSWER

If you go to a success workshop, walk through fire at a stadium event, or just plow your way through the usual "high performance" reading lists, your takeaway on intention may go something like this: Intention is your big, bold, hairy, audacious, ridiculously important vision. Intention is not just a desire. It's a *burning* desire. It infects you to your core. You know what you want, and you know, without question, how the world can and should be changed. You lack no conviction. Get it, proclaim it, kick off your shoes, and hit those hot coals, baby!

Okay, fine. This approach has indeed worked for some. But for the rest of us, it makes intention feel a lot like fast food—a quick grab from a neon menu and a supersized bag of instant fulfillment. Then, when you leave the event, you'll likely struggle to sustain that all-consuming drive. Sure, you got a cool iPhone photo of yourself barefoot on smoldering embers, but no real change to hang your hat on.

If you're one of those people who can't instantly locate your purpose, your passion, your reason for existing, your ambition, or your undaunted levels of certainty, you may be wondering if something is wrong with you.

Nothing is wrong with you.

Consider this. The rush of the moment—whether found in a book or at an event—can push people to "think big!" out of thin air. The pressure is on! Find your vision! Is it a big business? Dude. Crush it! Is it a million bucks? Awesome! Crush that, too!

For many, intention just doesn't work that way.

For one thing, when it comes to desire, not everyone burns. Not every vision lights up the sky with "passion" with a capital P, followed by three exclamation points!!! Not every dream zips down the boulevard in a Lamborghini flashing a "Go Big or Go Home!" bumper sticker.

For some of us, intention speaks softly. It nudges. In fact, at first, your intention may come wobbling down the pike in a funky little gypsy wagon sporting a well-worn bumper sticker that says, "I wonder if . . ." This kind of intention needs space and care to evolve. Hit it too hard with your agendas and demands, and it'll make its lumbering exit into the unknown.

There aren't many models out there that honor this more subtle style. In the business world, we're expected to be "on" all the time. Too often, a coach barks, "Well, what do you want?" expecting a rapid-fire answer, as if intention should leap out like a soldier at the ready. In our haste to please and be good soldiers, we find ourselves barking back: "A multimillion-dollar empire!" "10× my client load!" "Scale and go big!" And these shouts are often not so much intention as they are feeble attempts at the right answer.

But intention isn't a "right" answer. It's not a quick grab. In fact, when we get too caught up in practical, get-'er-done thinking, we end up contorting an intention more than creating one.

When I was a year or two into my songwriting career, I caught the eye of a music executive who, oddly, liked me enough to want to help me but who also dismissed my audience—mostly women—as impractical. They weren't gonna "show me the money!"

To him, it was obvious what needed to happen. He wanted me to rework my music, my look, and my marketing to appeal to college guys, citing that this demographic spent more money than anyone on music. His methodology made perfect sense to him. Go where the market data proved profitable.

Believing he had the answers, I obeyed his orders and set my intention for a new, "more profitable" audience. For a full year, I tried to write songs that might appeal to this person I wasn't remotely connected to. I made posters and publicity designed for the twenty-year-old male. The posters were cool. The songs were horrible. And the rest of it made me feel like a prostitute.

Then one evening I was performing at a college auditorium. As I was about to play my final song, a girl raised her hand. She stood up and shouted so everyone in the audience could hear. She shared with all of us that she'd been very emotional that day, and said it was probably because of her period, which began yesterday. (True story, I swear.) She said my music made her feel okay for the first time all week. She just wanted me to know that she was grateful. Then she sat down and blushed as her friends in the surrounding seats poked her and laughed.

And there it is, I thought.

This quirky girl who has netted a collective eye roll from the entire audience. This girl who is a bit too sensitive and tries to manage an oncoming wave of emotions on any given day at any given hour. The very one who won't drink enough beer for the club owners of the world to get all hopped up when I come to town. The one whose behavior at that moment would make my music-executive friend snort with derision. These are my peeps. It's not the college guy who spends all the money. It's her—who shared her menstrual cycle with two hundred people in a dark theater. She is who I am wired to make music for.

An intention was shaped into existence that night. I stopped enslaving myself to market data and let my calling create my intention instead.

Here's the simple way I define intention: Intention is desire, dream, or destiny fused with energy, attention, focus, and direction. As such, intention evolves. It doesn't come in a neatly typed five- or ten-year vision. How could it? Things change too quickly in business these days. So, all that long-term, left-brain, "here's my data-supported intention" is not only useless, but a little ridiculous in the twenty-first century.

Intention asks only this: What are you creating in your business now? And it doesn't demand a quick answer. It asks you to relax and consider what's evolving here, what's coming out of this business—and this heart—of yours.

When you set an intention, you're aligning the truest parts of yourself with your business. The doubts and shouts of others and your mind may slow down the ride or require some attention, but they don't get to determine what you want or who you become.

5

HOW IT STARTS: THE TWO DRIVERS OF INTENTION

ntention—whether it's about your ideal client, your next hire, or your entire business vision—can reveal itself in unexpected ways, using all kinds of unpredictable methods. So as you begin to ask yourself what you want to manifest now, it might help to know there are two drivers that initiate intention. And to understand which one is at work for you.

DRIVER #1: INTENTION FROM—WHEN YOU CAN NO LONGER DEAL WITH YOUR CURRENT SITUATION

The single line that has launched many an entrepreneurial venture goes something like this: "You gotta be kidding me."

Thinking back to the circumstances that finally drove me to the page where I wrote that first letter to God, I realize that my shitty cubicle job was quite the catalyst. The pain it produced forced me to get clear about the path I didn't want to travel, so I could bravely enter the one I was meant to take.

Sometimes that's how intention works, especially if we haven't yet built a strong relationship with our intuition. If you don't yet trust the quiet voice of your intuition, your life will find other, often louder, ways to speak to you. As a festering problem or discomfort pushes you out of your apathy, a better idea emerges or is created. That's how "Intention From" works. The intention is born out of undesired circumstances.

I know Law of Attraction junkies everywhere will revolt at this idea, citing the belief that your negative thoughts will taint your energy. That *not* wanting something places your attention squarely on the thing not wanted, therefore creating more of the unwanted thing. My experience has proven otherwise.

Again and again I've seen frustrations become great incentives. They shape us. They teach us who we really are. We bump up against an edge, it hurts, and we find another way. Think of a maze from a children's book or magazine. You move your pencil along the path until you reach . . . what? A dead end! The dead end leaves you with no choice but to find another path, one that feels more possible. Ultimately—because of these stops and even a few false starts—you reach your goal.

The movement away from something often sparks the initial desire for change that creates a new outcome.

- We're bored in our corporate job, so we take our skill set and head out on our own.
- We're sick of being broke, so we downsize our lives, go part-time in our job, and build a small side business.
- The "up-and-coming" neighborhood we live in keeps not coming up like the real estate agent promised, so we create a vision for the perfect house elsewhere.

These and other reaction-based intentions get us going. They catalyze a new direction.

DRIVER #2: INTENTION TOWARD—WHEN YOU HAVE A BRILLIANT IDEA AND KNOW WHAT YOU WANT

When my client Sue Ludwig was a neonatal therapist working in a hospital, the same idea kept popping into her head: Someone should create an association for neonatal therapists. The idea wouldn't go away. It followed her home at night. It went with her to the medical conferences she attended. It arose every time a nurse dismissed a therapist's practices as "unscientific."

When she finally initiated that intention by becoming the "someone who should" and taking the first action steps, all kinds of doors opened. That's how she ended up on that stage just four years later—and every year thereafter—addressing the hundreds of people she'd brought together to improve care for premature babies worldwide.

This can happen to anyone hit by an idea like *I wonder if I could*, or *Wouldn't it be cool if*, or *You know, someone should really*. Let's be honest. Most people get great ideas and do nothing about them. They let the idea wander off to someone else's eager mind. After all, it'd be lots of work to create that. But this is where initiating intention builds clear energy around an idea. You simply start by saying yes to the idea, reiterating "I'm In," and then opening up to next steps.

Sue says that once she said yes to her idea, a weird thing happened. She went from thinking, *Someone should start an association for neonatal therapists*, to thinking, *I hope no one else gets the idea to start an association for neonatal therapists*. She'd made it her own.

When Intention Toward is your driver, you initiate based on what you want to create, not on what you are moving away from. It requires a higher level of clarity and energy, and a willingness to dive headfirst into the territory of uncertainty and curiosity.

Starting with Intention From is like climbing into a raft and sitting backward, facing the land you're leaving behind. You have to keep that strong reference point to where you were, letting your unwillingness to go back motivate you. Then, when you're ready, you get to turn around, face the direction you're heading, and start scanning for land. When you begin with Intention Toward, you hop on that raft facing forward, not really sure of the course, but knowing that land will appear eventually.

To sustain a successful business, Intention From must eventually grow into Intention Toward. But either is a good place to start. No matter which way you're facing on that raft, at least you're saying "yes" to something better. After that, how you make your intention come to life is up to you.

SOME CLARITY ON CLARITY

I can't count the number of people who have shown up at my events, stood at the microphone, and announced that they want "clarity." "Clarity on my message!" "Clarity on my purpose!" "Clarity on my ideal client!" "Clarity on my next steps!"

Especially when it comes to initiating intention, clarity is the ingredient everyone's craving. But what *is* clarity? What is this thing we want so bad? And, most importantly, why don't we seem to have any?

The way I see it, clarity is a way of life. It's a state of being. When you experience its impact in one facet of your business, it becomes a nonnegotiable. You'll covet it in all areas.

The problem is we're not used to clarity. It gets whittled away throughout our lives by "shoulds," judgments, shame, and all the tiny pressures that make us question ourselves and stop trusting our instincts or desires. Social conditioning is the magnet that has messed up our clarity compass. We're trained to be pulled and ruled by other people's agendas and opinions.

Time and again, we find ourselves ever so delicately exiting the zone of "What I Want" (our intention) and slipping into the zone of "What I Think I Can Get" without realizing what's happening. Clarity is shoved aside. Instead of stretching, we settle. Instead of persisting, we muddle. When this pattern continues long enough, the intender ends up telling everyone the most classic story of all: "I don't know what I want. I'm not clear." Because they don't. And they aren't.

This is how clarity becomes so mysterious. It gets buried. We forget it's even an option.

Renee, a corporate trainer and executive coach, had set an intention to stop working nights and weekends, a result of the many interruptions that distracted her from her client work. After going through several Uplevel You trainings on sales sequences, Renee got clarity on exactly how her sales process would work to eliminate the time-consuming back-and-forth she typically engaged in with prospects. This included a simple step where prospects themselves would go online and schedule a "Get Acquainted" call with Renee, choosing from a calendar of pre-set times. This single change would free up hours of her time each week.

Within days of setting up the sequence, it started working. Three people had scheduled themselves and were ready to roll. Then Renee got a message on LinkedIn. The writer opened by stating she didn't particularly like Renee's online scheduler. She couldn't find a time that worked for her. So she gave Renee a time, stating it was her only option.

Renee didn't want to be rude. She didn't want to lose a potential client. And even though she felt like she was under attack, she ignored her new-found clarity, messaged the woman back, and confirmed the appointment for the next morning.

At eight sharp, Renee sat at her desk preparing for the conversation when the woman messaged again, canceling the call. Last minute "stuff" had come up.

While this is a lesson in communicating boundaries and requiring prospects to do homework before they even get on a call with you, at its core, it's a lesson in clarity. Clarity isn't just a nice idea. Being clear requires that the owner of said clarity embodies that clarity, practicing it, living it.

That means that clarity—for our purposes—is a verb. Clarity reveals itself bit by bit as our experiences in life and business ask us if we're more committed to "shoulds" and opinions than we are to our own clarity.

After the disappointment of the thoughtless cancellation, Renee recommitted to her clarity. She saw this incident for exactly what it was: a soul expansion. What this woman's actions conveyed to Renee was: *This is what happens when you're not clear*. It also let Renee experience in real time that clarity is not about being rude by refusing to budge from a set system. It's about staying committed to your intention because you know what's best for you (and your peeps).

6

HOW WE KILL INTENTION

When I first moved away from home to forge a life as a performer and songwriter, I got many letters from my parents. These were not happy letters. They were warning letters.

Mind you, I don't come from a family of entrepreneurs or artists. In my parents' attempts to protect me from tossing myself into a life of poverty and suffering, they regularly let me know I was making the wrong choice. My dad told me, on several occasions, I was going "downhill." My mom wrote that there was "only one Mary Chapin Carpenter." (My idol, who I apparently didn't measure up to.)

Whenever I got one of these letters, I went fetal. They terrified me. They went to work in my mind and tried to get me to shrink my intention, or just plain give up. Get the cubicle job and be satisfied with a few rounds of "Uncle John's Band" in Sunday-night song circles.

But then one day, I heard one of those often-told Zen stories. It's an old tale about a seeker who'd traveled many miles by foot to a monastery, ready to begin his devotion in earnest.

When he finally arrived at the entry gate, he was asked, "What do you want?"

"I want truth," he replied.

He was told to go away. The door was slammed in his face.

He sat outside in the cold overnight.

The next day, the door opened a crack. He was asked again what he wanted. He made his intention clear. They said to go away.

Yet another slamming door.

Still, he sat. In the rain. In the cold. With no food. Day after day, he was told to go away. But he stayed. Until finally, one day, the door opened, and he was welcomed in. His clarity had been proven. His intention was real.

When I heard this story, I thought, *Oh, so these letters are just the monastery door!* I began to see any adversity, be it rejection, criticism, inner doubt, or confusion, simply as clarity's way of poking me. Checking in. Giving me the opportunity to stand more firmly in my intention. Or providing me with a seemingly sensible (and convenient) excuse to exit the scene. It was all so inconspicuous, and I marveled at how easy it was to be misled.

People often lean toward the dramatic when talking about what gets in the way of intention. Even in initial conversations about intention, you'll hear words like "sabotage" get tossed around. As in, "I always sabotage my own success!" As if they're waging a war against evil, and the dark forces are winning out with a space station that can blast entire planets to oblivion.

But it's never like that, is it? And unless you're a five-star military strategist, "sabotage" is mostly a stupid word. What keeps you from taking action is never that obvious, never that big, and never that dangerous. Our obstacles aren't Darth Vader entering the scene with all that metallic heavy breathing, the shiny helmet, and the ominous theme song composed by John Williams.

Our obstacles are fleeting, like the sharp sound of a door closing in your face. They're rational, like the fact that there really *is* only one Mary Chapin Carpenter. They're even practical, like how running an errand is more urgent than sitting at your desk and facing your latest blog post, which by anyone's standards could've been written by your dog.

In fact, the primary blocks to intention are subtle. You barely notice them until they've orchestrated all of your moves and caused their desired end result: you, stuck in place. In my coaching work, I've discovered that the obstacles to intention can fit neatly into three categories: waiting, rushing, and blinging.

1. THE INTENTION KILLER THAT PRETENDS TO BE A VERB: WAITING

It's every speaker's nightmare. (Okay, it's probably just *my* nightmare. But let's say it's yours, too.) That one person in the front row with the cold, beady eyes and the frozen smirk that never breaks, not even when you're at your funniest. Arms crossed over their rib cage. Posture seething, screaming, "I don't buy a thing you're saying." And there you are, the speaker, becoming target practice for their steely gaze as you traverse back and forth in front of the room.

On this particular evening, this stance was held by a graphic designer named Charlotte. Her cynical energy filled the air, making me stumble and stammer through the content, which was all about getting clarity on your ideal client.

I stopped. I took a deep breath and a sip of water.

"Charlotte," I said. "What's up?"

Charlotte looked around, now a spokesperson for the others. She was rallying the troops. It was her moment. All eyes were on her.

"You know," she said. "I think I speak for everyone here. All this 'clarity' stuff . . . " She paused to do air quotes. "It's kinda manipulation, you know? I'm a go-with-the-flow kind of girl. What's wrong with 'surrender'? For me, the clients who show up, show up. If it doesn't work out, then I know it's not the will of the Universe."

Charlotte looked around, pleased at the nods she saw.

I decided to take a moment to ask Charlotte about her business.

Charlotte had been running her design business on the side for three years and was still holding a full-time job. She'd been fired by her last client after a miscommunication and resulting blowup. (She was still trying to "let this go.") She wasn't enjoying her work as a graphic designer and was getting, in her words, "a message from the Universe" that maybe she wasn't meant to be one.

I asked her, "So, Charlotte, why did you start this business in the first place?"

She shrugged. Then she said, "Because I love it. And I thought I could turn it into my full-time thing."

"What do you love about it?" I asked.

She looked up at the ceiling. "To me, design is everything. I love when the design makes people light up." Charlotte's energy shifted. "And I love getting lost in the creating of it—and all of the subtle changes that make the graphics better and better. There's like this magical thing that happens."

"Are you good at it?" I asked.

She smiled. Her first real smile of the evening. "I'm *really* good at it."

"So then," I said. "Why would an intelligent Universe be sending you 'messages' that you aren't meant to be a graphic designer?"

Charlotte's eyes shot downward. "I don't know," she said almost inaudibly. "Maybe it wasn't meant to be." Tears filled her eyes. "I mean, I keep waiting for a sign that it's okay to pursue this thing. But it just keeps being hard."

This is when I ditched my notes on ideal clients and focused instead on this insidious intention block known as "Waiting."

Initiating intention—whether that's identifying your ideal client, or structuring your pricing, or starting a business at all—can feel aggressive and scary. When it comes time to make a move, we wonder if we really have the smarts, the ability, or even the right to bring our intention into the world. So rather than live through our discomfort and risk failure, we turn our clarity over to something outside of us.

Then we wait for that something before we do anything.

Charlotte had decided to turn over her clarity about her ideal client and even her whole business to "the Universe." She'd decided to *surrender*.

Now, before you start telling me about your daily yoga practice and how you've learned to surrender, and how surrender is spiritual, and how your favorite book *ever* is about "letting go," and how we all need to surrender, I urge you to pay attention. I get it. Surrender is a necessary part of owning a business, having relationships, or living a life. And, yes, there are those who live in a state of surrender, in the present moment at all times. Some call this enlightenment. I don't pretend to know.

What I do know is that more often than not, especially in business, a scared little ego hears about this lofty thing called "surrender," and then co-opts it for its own purposes. It uses the irresistible idea of surrender as a spiritually correct way to avoid a holy host of uncomfortable things—namely the fear intention brings up, along with the clarity and self-awareness it demands. This is how the righteous vibe of "go with the flow" conveniently deflects any challenge and becomes the perfect place to hide from being a creator in your business and life.

So you "wait for signs" from the Universe, convinced that you've surrendered to a higher power. But you're really just avoiding discomfort, looking high and low for a signal you can translate into the "go-ahead" you need.

Waiting, whether for a circumstance, an event, some cash, or a person, is always about one thing: giving your inner power to something outside of yourself. Technically, "to wait" is a verb. But really, it just keeps you frozen in place in a very un-verb-like way. When you wait, you become an object waiting for a subject to come along and convince you to move.

And there are all kinds of reasons people wait. Some people wait for permission. As if there's some divine principal's office handing out hall passes. Some wait for credibility, accumulating degree after degree or tirelessly seeking just one more certification. Others wait for perfection, for a more refined and less damaged version of themselves to show up before they'll even entertain the idea of initiating an intention. Still others wait for discovery. Looking for someone with status and sparkle—perhaps Oprah (but Tim Ferriss would do)—to see all of their potential and turn them into a big star without having to get mired in all that messy clarity stuff.

They're all just waiting for that ultimate illusion: certainty. That's why we busy ourselves making list after list of pros and cons. Or why we go on opinion-gathering missions, hitting up our friends for their take. ("What do *you* think of my intention?") And why we dive headlong into a sea of statistics, data, and research to prove our point. ("Fifty-eight percent of all businesses failed last year!")

The thing about intention is it's deeper than a mental process. The thing about friends is they want your safety more than your expansion. And the thing about statistics and data is that none of it can tell you how many of those people who "failed" at business got lost in an epic Netflix binge weeks after they got home from the chamber of commerce with their new DBA certificate, or, alternatively, which of them learned from their failure and went on to create something hugely successful two years later. In the end, it's all just delaying clarity on your intention.

Those who wait rarely call it "waiting," however. They're so mired in the pattern, they don't see it. Instead, they say practical, obvious phrases like, "I'm a go-with-the-flow kind of gal." Or, "I'm getting necessary certifications first." Or, "I'm digging into the data before I make a move." And if you're like 99 percent of the people on this planet, you nod and say, "Of course you are! That makes total sense. You go, girl."

The reason the Universe doesn't give you the sign, the permission isn't granted, and certainty doesn't make an appearance is because—at its core—intention is a call. It calls you into a relationship with your own power. And you don't get to bypass this part. You don't get to be passive. Intention calls you to make the first move, which is exactly what I said to Charlotte about her ideal client and her ability to build a business. "What if the Universe is waiting for *you* to take the first step here? To intend? To get clear? And what if once you do that, the Universe takes a step toward you because it finally knows what you want?"

"Intention is not about control or aggression or manipulation," I continued. "Sure, there's wisdom in 'go with the flow.' Just be cognizant that 'go with the flow' doesn't mean 'have no strategy.' It doesn't mean don't get clear on who you best serve or how you serve them. It doesn't mean don't initiate an intention."

When I finished sharing all this with Charlotte, I stood still. I was curious to see where she would take it. This isn't always easy to hear.

Within seconds, Charlotte was wiping the tears away. She even smiled again.

"I'm so busted," she said.

2. THE DRIVE-BY INTENTION KILLER: RUSHING

You might be feeling superior right about now. Maybe you read through all that stuff about waiting and even scoffed a little. "Waiting? Um, no. I don't wait. I dive right in."

Of course you do. Your style is not so much defined by the brake pedal as it is the gas pedal. In fact, just this weekend, you were at a seminar and heard one of the speakers—a business guru—say, "If you don't have time, you need a team." So, you thought to yourself, *Well yeah. I never have time. I'm gonna hire an assistant first thing on Monday.* (There. An intention, right?)

So now it's Monday, and you click through about six or so other local ads for assistants, cutting and pasting their copy into your ad. You check out what they're paying and to be on the safe side, you offer fifty cents more per hour. Ha. Your ad is complete. You post it Tuesday morning.

On Tuesday afternoon, you get three replies in your in-box. Score! You set up a phone interview with one of them.

On Wednesday, you do the phone interview. She seems nice. She likes border collies. (You have two!) And hey, she's a Leo. (Just like you!)

So, you meet her at Starbucks on Thursday. And, man, you guys totally click. She seems to know her way around the internet. She's into social media. She says she's all about helping people. (You *love* that she's all about helping people—especially since you need so much help!) You hire her on the spot. (Look at you! You've got your first assistant! You got this intention stuff down.)

She starts on Monday. She's a bit slow to learn, but you both really like each other. By Wednesday, you notice she doesn't seem to catch on quickly. By Friday, *WTF*, she just sits around waiting for you to tell her what to do. She's not at all like those "A Players" that the business guru talked about in your seminar! She's not asking the right questions—or *any* questions for that matter. And you had to give her a lesson in Excel. The next Monday, she disappears for two hours at lunch. The next Tuesday, she calls in sick. And on and on. Until you have to let her go. She gets defensive, accuses you of being the worst boss she's ever had, and storms out of your home office slamming doors, leaving you totally shaken.

RIP first assistant. And as far as you're concerned, RIP this intention stuff.

So sure, you don't wait. You make shit happen. But in this case? That's about *all* you made happen.

For one thing, you didn't actually initiate your own intention. You let the seminar speaker do it. When he made the kicky remark about needing a team, you instantly took it to mean "hire someone now"—like tomorrow.

If we're being honest, you didn't initiate *that* intention either. You cut and pasted together the intentions of six other businesses and sent them out into the world as your own. So, is it surprising that the wrong person with the wrong skill set showed up at your business for the wrong job?

No. Because you rushed. You saw a ready-made, fast-food intention, grabbed it, and took off. No questions asked. No thoughts explored. None of that unpleasant dirty work that forces you to examine the muck of your business or your mindset.

I call this "the Drive-By Intention." Though it seems like something of substance—what with all that activity and everything—it's really nothing more than an attempt to avoid another call of intention, the call to clarity, the opportunity to assess your current situation and consider what your business is asking for.

I get it, though. As business owners, our days get busy. Time is precious. Our lives become all about the work in front of us, surviving, getting through one task and onto the next. You think: *Clarity schmarity, I have a hundred emails to answer.*

So when we come across an idea that promises to make our lives easier—like having a team, or a million bucks, or even "lifestyle design"—it's tempting to just grab it, make it our intention, and keep driving, leaving clarity and our true intention (the one that can take us where we really want to go) in the dust by the side of the road.

A Drive-By Intention means we don't think. We react on impulse. And that keeps us skating on the surface level, never going more than skin-deep with our intention. Sure, we want clarity, and we even have a crush on intention. But they demand so much from us. So, we avoid doing the work to attain them. With no clarity and no clear intention, we find ourselves in an inauthentic business held together by duct tape.

3. THE BRIGHT SHINY INTENTION KILLER: EGO BLING

One morning, days after I made my bold move and gave my two-week notice at Ogilvy & Mather, I was in the Ford dealership service department getting my Escort repaired.

The head mechanic, Phil, handed me a long intake form that included fields for name, date, phone, address, Social Security number, and, then, there it was . . . a blank field with the label "Employer."

In that moment, I didn't remember my clear intention of becoming a songwriter. I didn't remember all those letters to God. I didn't even know what a dream was.

In that moment, the "Employer" field sent me into an identity crisis. Without that prestigious employer name to back me up, who was I? Strangers would no longer find me impressive, or even worthy. Farewell raised eyebrows. Hello blank stares.

My heart pounded. My breathing became shallow. I was having a mini panic attack under the green glow of the fluorescent lights while four people behind me waited their turn.

Here's where you—ever the rational thinker when it comes to other people's lives—might say, "Wait a minute, Christine. You're willing to turn your back on your dreams and your future so that Phil, the head mechanic at Koons Ford in Fairfax, Virginia, will look at your service contract and find you impressive?"

"Yes," I'd say, "that's exactly what's happening here."

I've seen clients cling to bigger and smaller imaginary items at similar moments of intention. Their "Regional Director" title. Their club membership. The company car. The special treatment they get at the airline counter because they earn so many frequent flier miles going on business trips they despise. Their Platinum status in the Marriott hotel chain. Or even a rent-controlled, shoebox-sized apartment on the Lower West Side that lets them feel somehow superior to all the suckers paying current New York City prices.

So, yes, at that particular moment, Phil was the gatekeeper of my entire identity. And no, it mattered not at all that he probably A) didn't care, B) had never heard of David Ogilvy, and C) (which is the most likely) never once read a word of these contracts.

Intention can feel like a threat to your very identity. Especially if you've accumulated a nice collection of "ego bling," the sole purpose of which is to prop up that identity with perceived status. This then becomes the high-stakes reason you can't move forward: the fear that you'll lose that phony, but reliable, sense of self.

Here we have the final call of intention: the call to choose what's *real*. What's *most* real here? Is it all this ego bling you cling to—whether or not you're perceived as special, important, or reputable by your mechanic or the night manager at the Chicago Ritz-Carlton? Or is it who you know to your core you're meant to become? How you answer this is everything.

Know this: Initiating intention and following through demands your energy. Sometimes it means you'll have to shed baggage that's been holding you back forever. Or you'll have to say no. Or some people won't like the choices you make. Or they won't like *you*. Some of those people will walk away. Others will tell you you're nuts. Others, still, will tell you your intention won't work.

While it can at times feel as if you're playing a game of Whac-A-Mole with intention blocks, the true game is all about awareness. Witness all the ways your mind and ego find to play tricks on you, not only with intention but in every stage of the Soul Track. Then understand that you can let these derail you (as you always have) or you can use them as opportunities to break a pattern and anchor more deeply to your intention, to get clearer.

Even the smallest of intentions can unearth these blocks. It's why so many people settle for bad employees and say yes to invitations they have zero interest in. Clarity can feel like a real effort when you're face-to-face with unconscious forces that have, up to this point, ruled your life.

Consistently being clear so you make decisions that support your intention is a nonnegotiable part of your job as an entrepreneur. When we use the practice of intention as a way to build a strong relationship with our clarity, we not only build strong businesses, but we become powerful creators. And that's an endless source of confidence.

YOUR BIG WHY AND YOUR BIG EGO

Once upon a time, I tried to get rid of my ego.

I was a few years into my music career, and I realized that I had some lovely reasons for becoming a performer. I wanted to inspire people. I wanted people to feel uplifted the way I felt uplifted when I left concerts.

But alongside that stuff, I discovered these embarrassing, prom-queen-like motivations. They said things like, "Screw inspiration. I want approval!" It was clear these voices were every bit a part of my motivation as my more noble intentions.

So, I stopped touring. I stopped calling promoters. I stopped mailing anything to my list, telling myself I was taking a break in order to deepen my approach to creativity and business. Which sounded much better than the truth, which was that I wanted to destroy my ego and never be needy again.

How'd that work out for you, Christine?

Well, needless to say, if I'd waited for this to happen, I'd still be sitting on my IKEA couch, reading Eckhart Tolle and eating kale chips.

Enter a wise, older business owner and former actor who became sort of a mentor to me.

He asked me to open up to the possibility that I was allowed to bring all the parts of myself along for the ride. My noble, wise self with her altruistic intentions. And my needy, grasping, approval-seeking self who just wanted people to clap for me.

The two could live side by side.

"The trick," he told me, "is to not hand the keys to the bus over to the needy one. Make sure that one never gets to drive."

This epiphany irritated me. I wanted a more enlightened version of myself to show up before I did anything else ever. I never wanted to feel pain, envy, shame, jealousy, or worthlessness again . . . and enlightenment felt like a good way out of these things. Sort of like a spiritual martini.

I slowly learned, however, that purpose, soul, and truth are what you discover by taking action and letting yourself experience this unwanted dark side.

When Dustin Hoffman was on *Inside the Actors Studio*, he shared a conversation he and Laurence Olivier had over dinner when they finished making the movie *Marathon Man*. Hoffman was a young actor, and at the end of the meal he asked Olivier, "Tell me. What's the reason we do what we do?"

In a flash, Olivier got up, stood by Hoffman, and said, "You want to know why, dear boy?" And without a second's pause, Olivier leaned over into the young actor's face and whispered, "*Look at me! Look at me! Look at me! Look at me! Look at me! Look at me! Look at me!*"

I love this.

I love it because it's freedom. It's freedom at a time when we're told almost daily to "Have a Big Why!" We're instructed to "Change the World!" We're given hierarchies of "pure emotions vs. base emotions," and we're informed that if we're not 100 percent about motivating people, then we should quit until we are.

Well, a little acceptance of your ego voices goes a long way to making you clear, even agile. So let's make an agreement right now. Go ahead and have your Big Why. Make a bold intention. But don't give in to these weird repressed Calvinist messages of purity and egoless-ness.

That's all just ego, too!

Think about it.

Your spiritual self isn't thinking, *Get that fucking ego out of my way so I can be spiritual already!* No. This whole hatred of ego *is* ego. It's just the ego trying to sweep itself under the rug. And in that way, it keeps you focused on ego, which is its whole goal in the first place.

So bring along your fear, neediness, anxiety, grasping, or even "look at me." (I won't tell a soul.) Sometimes these are the very prompts we need to get things going in the first place.

Just make sure those parts ride shotgun. Don't give them the keys to the bus, okay?

7

INITIATING YOUR INTENTION

G o!" she shouted. I stood still. "Go on!" She shoved me forward.

"Really?" I said, turning to look at her.

She was laughing now. "They're still cheering, stupid! Go!"

When the promoter of the show pushes you back to the stage for your second encore, you do it. Even if you just did your first encore. Even if you're not the headline act. Even if you're wondering if this is really happening.

So I did. I walked back out on stage. In the breezy air of a warm summer evening when the sun was just about to set, the crowd of thousands stood up from their blankets and folding chairs on the lawn and cheered. Sure, they weren't there for me precisely. This much I knew. They were there for the headliners. My very first CD had been released a few months before, and this was my first big moment as an opening act. I was unknown. (Well, maybe a little less unknown now.)

The lawn got quiet as I stepped up to the mic. A whistle sang out somewhere toward the back of the crowd. Then a shout. I took a moment to tune my guitar and reminded myself to breathe. Just as I was about to play my encore song, I heard a voice somewhere inside me say simply, "Let this in."

I took a deep breath and did just that. The stage lights glowed in the evening air and felt warm on my skin. The drum set behind me magnified their colors in its metallic shine. The breeze blew my hair. And the stage monitors, custom tweaked for my ears by skillful sound engineers, let me hear my guitar effortlessly as I tuned.

This was the real deal. I wasn't standing in the corner of a bar or on a rickety side stage at a street festival. This was what I had dreamed of, *more* than I had dreamed of, just three and a half years earlier, when I first had the audacity to take a deeply buried dream and turn it into an intention.

For a brief moment, because this is how my mind works, I didn't want to play my song. I wanted to say to the audience, "You do realize how insane it is that I'm even standing on this stage, right?"

I smiled to myself at all of it—the intention, the path it was taking me on, this moment. There would be more ups and downs, but for now, I did as the voice asked me to do: I let this sink in. And I played my second encore song.

THE INTENTIONIZER TOOL

Intention works. But it asks for work back from you. And as we've talked about all along, that work begins with clarity. *Your* clarity. The Intentionizer Tool below tunes you into your awareness, allowing you to see and bring clarity to your whole amazing, confusing, creative self. By putting that effort in now—thinking through what you want and don't want, and where fear, ego, or negative thoughts might stop you—you start a powerful creative process. So honor your dreams and take your time moving through these steps.

Step #1: Intention Toward. Describe your dream or intention.

Imperfectly (and playfully, if possible) describe what your intention looks like, how it feels, and what it is. Keep in mind that clarity is key no matter how big or small your intention. Maybe you want to build a team to support you. Maybe you want to host an event. Maybe you want to finally start your coaching business. Write it in long form, short form, bullet points, whatever. It doesn't have to be perfect prose or move anyone to tears. Just get it down on paper.

Step #2: Intention From. List up to five things you don't want.

If the first step has you stumped, think about what you don't want in your life anymore—unmotivated employees, housework, clients who want quick fixes. Writing out what you don't want can give you the kick-start you need to see what you do want. For many of us this "Intention From" step is our first, and very necessary, step to forming an "Intention Toward." So make a list of situations you'd like to say goodbye to. They don't have to be major. When you're done, look at the list. What would it take to solve the item that bothers you most or change it into what you do want? There's your intention.

Step #3: Once you settle on what you want, write down three good or "noble" reasons why you want this thing or circumstance.

This is the fun part. These are the cool reasons—the lofty and poetic reasons—you want this thing. Like "serving people," or "making the world better," or "righting a wrong." This is what you would say right off the bat if someone asked you why you want this. These reasons are true and real and exciting.

Step #4: Now list three "ego" reasons.

In *The Empire Strikes Back*, Yoda sends Luke Skywalker into a cave where Luke ends up face-to-face with himself as Darth Vader. This is a little like that. These reasons are what you wouldn't readily admit if asked why you want this intention. They aren't the stuff of a noble Jedi, but more like: "to make boatloads of money," "to be admired," or "to one-up my Lexus-driving, Wall Street, tool-of-a-brother-in-law at the next reunion."

Why do this? For the same reason as Luke (and every other hero, warrior, shaman, or mystic)—because you no longer want these darker motives operating in the background. Awareness is your new superpower. Pretending you don't have an ego doesn't make it go away. No matter how altruistic you convince yourself you are and how far down you stuff those ego reasons, when you face a tough choice, they'll resurface—each and every time—and assign themselves a prominent position in your decision-making process. And when you make tough choices from your unconscious ego, rooted in some old story and supported by fear, you often end up with a business that's not at all what you wanted or intended.

So expose them now. Write them down. Celebrate your awareness of them, knowing you are doing the work of the warrior.

Step #5: List up to five changes you may have to make.

Everyone wants transformation. But very few want to do what it takes to transform. For instance, many solo business owners begin their work with me with the intention to grow their revenue to six figures when they've been stuck at the $45K mark for years. This increase almost always means they'll have to make changes in their pricing, their team, their ideal client, or their mindset. And that can get uncomfortable.

So consider that when you initiate intention, change will be part of the deal. This step will set the groundwork to prepare you.

List up to five changes you may have to make—internally or externally—as your intention manifests.

Step #6: Are you "In"?

Pause for a moment. This is a big deal. Review what you've written. Especially review the changes you may have to make. Then, ask yourself: "Am I In?" See what the answer is. Yes? Or no? If you're not feeling energized, then take another look at it. Is it something you really want? Take your time and tweak as needed. When you know you're committed and "In," write the words, "I'm In!" at the bottom of your page and add your signature.

To download a supremely cool printable copy of the Intentionizer and other tools in this book, visit www.SoulSourcedBook.com.

Bonus Step: Become your intention at random moments.

This bonus step is a playful but powerful exercise that takes your intention out of the mind and allows it to enter your whole being. You embody it. When you become your intention, you use your powerful imagination, at random moments in your day, to simply be the person who has already manifested and embodied this intention.

For instance, let's say you're walking into Trader Joe's, about to squeeze through the aisles in your usual rushed fashion. Instead, you pause. You consider your intention of having the ideal operations director running all the tedious elements of your business. You imagine the serenity this outcome brings you. How does this peaceful entrepreneur move through the grocery store? Can you get a sense of how this intention changes who you are and how you behave? It's a little bit like trying on a new outfit. A new way of being. Walk around in it. What does it feel like? What's different? What's the same? Every intention has a flavor to it, and only you can experience what that is.

To wrap up the process, sit with things. When you've completed the Intentionizer, put your answers away for seven days. This will create space for your responses to get traction and start to connect. When you feel ready, review everything you wrote and add any new insights that have come up. If necessary, look at this tool again and redo.

Give yourself ample space and time for this and know that initiating an intention is always an evolving process—not an arrival. Be flexible with your answers.

8

WHAT TO DO IF YOU DON'T KNOW WHAT YOU WANT

This is unbearable," Rachel said. "I mean, I always know what I want. And now I don't, and it's freaking me out!"

There's a pattern that can slowly take hold in a business without the owner even spotting it. I call it "the Cycle of Reactivity and Panic." (Or, more appropriately, "C.R.A.P.") The cycle starts when things slow down and the business owner gets scared. She reacts. She frantically makes calls and sends emails, doing anything to "drum up some business" without any strategy or intention. The only aim is to make enough money to get by for the next month or two or three or who cares? It doesn't matter, as long as *someone* is paying her *something*.

When her frenetic efforts pay off, she enters the "panic" phase. She's so busy with a load of non-ideal clients and jobs that she's working weekends and nights with no support staff. In this phase, she says things like, "By the time I show someone what to do, I could just do it myself," which means she never hires that someone, especially since she doesn't have a clue how long this client load will last. Of course, it *doesn't* last because she doesn't have time to continue her marketing efforts. That's when she reacts all over again.

When a business is in this cycle for too long, the owner can't find her vision anymore. Her stress is running the show, and she has forgotten how intention works. Everything has become about survival. When driven by survival, intention just leads to more ideas about how to survive.

Rachel had been in this cycle for two years. She was so used to it, so burnt out, that she couldn't find the space to consider her intention, to ask herself what she wanted this business to be. Or what she wanted at all.

She had hired a local business coach who fired her in two months, telling her to come back to him when she had some kind of a goal.

Now she was on the phone with me. She showed up for our first call determined not to get fired, putting her best face on the whole situation. She was armed with all kinds of goals and intentions for where her business could go. But her goals felt lifeless. When I confronted her about this, she stopped the game playing and admitted the truth.

"I don't know what I want. I mostly just don't want to be tired anymore. Is that a goal?" she laughed.

"Well, it's a start," I said. "Let's see if you can reconnect with your clarity, as you keep the business running without so much panic."

"Not knowing" isn't a desired state in conventional business-growth strategy. But I've been in that state. My clients have, too. I bet you have as well. In my experience, the number-one worst thing you can do when you find yourself "not knowing" is to push or prod. Because you'll hear yourself making up fake intentions, spouting off goals that sound great but aren't true. Then you're off and running, creating something completely out of alignment when you're already tired.

The terror of not knowing what you want (and especially admitting this) can be palpable. We'll do anything to avoid facing that emptiness. Sometimes, though, that's exactly what we need to do. To be with it. To let it reveal, as it always does, not just what *we* want next, but what our souls want next, and what our businesses need next.

My neighbor Bramlett is a masterful gardener. Visitors to my home always ask about "the house down the street." The one they saw as they drove in. The one with the amazing gardens. It's tempting to think that Bramlett and his partner are driving around buying plants every day, digging things up, mapping out plans, and busily making it all happen.

But that's not how it works. In fact, if you watched Bramlett in action, you'd catch him, more often than not, standing perfectly still. Just being in the space and staring at, well, nothing in particular. The act of being with emptiness. The act of not knowing. Strangely enough, that's how you end up knowing. By standing still, taking it all in, and paying attention, Bramlett gets clear on the balance and artistry of the landscape—the textures and the colors.

Years ago, I had ended a relationship and moved out of a house into an apartment on my own. I didn't have any furniture. I was alone for the first time in years. As I sometimes do when I'm grasping for answers, I opened up a book and read the first sentence that caught my eye. That sentence was, "Live for a time empty." It was a phrase that kept me sane. It reminded me that empty is not only good, empty is necessary. So for months, I sat on folding chairs. I didn't have a sofa. I didn't have paintings on the walls. It was a little embarrassing, but much like Bramlett and his garden, the space itself began to reveal what it wanted. And slowly, the empty began to take shape and create a fullness that was alive and aligned.

Most people won't do this. They see a garden, they want it filled. Drive on down to Home Depot and pack your trunk with anything that claims to bloom. I've even shared my "live for a time empty" experience with friends who are stressing over furnishing a new home. But most people can't be with the empty. As soon as they get their house keys, they rush out to the furniture store and get stuff that fills the space. (Only to end up with items bound to appear on an "Intention From" list somewhere in the not-too-distant future.)

As a business coach, I deal with this same phenomenon. Maybe even more so. Business is supposed to be a place of certainty, even if you have to fake it. There's no room for "live for a time empty" in the fast-paced world of business success. Tell an entrepreneur to be with the space, and they instantly get visions of themselves pushing a shopping cart with all of their belongings down the city streets asking for handouts after their epic failure. They'll do anything to avoid that fear.

It's normal and natural to think, *I have to know. And I have to know now.* But there are times when we don't know, and we're not meant to know. This is a conscious not knowing. And being able to navigate the discomfort of this territory is one piece of being masterful at anything.

THE BREAKDOWN BEFORE THE BREAKTHROUGH: FOUR FLAVORS OF "I DON'T KNOW"

Not knowing what you want doesn't mean you get to collapse and be a drama queen. Action is still required. Struggle is not. If you don't know your intention right now, or if you're drawing a blank, don't force it. Instead, see if you can sense what's behind not knowing. There are four scenarios where not knowing is calling you to a deeper place.

1. You're not ready to know yet.

Sometimes our next move requires gestation time, or time for us to release things in order to create space to see through a belief we've outgrown. Make that space. Trust that this kind of not knowing calls for patience.

When a client is going through such times, my job as a coach is to hold the space for the new vision to be created. I've watched some clients grow resentful or filled with longing when they see others hit their goals and make so much happen. When these clients evolve out of that space, when they rediscover the vision or intention, what they create has much more authenticity, clarity, and meaning.

2. It's the first time you've ever truly asked yourself.

At one of my early retreats, during an exercise on clarity, I asked each participant to describe their intention. As the room started writing furiously, a woman named Melanie just sat staring. She seemed to be staring at me. But mostly she was just gazing, deer in headlights, into a void.

"Mel?" I whispered. "You okay?"

In her soft Southern accent, she said, "I'm just realizing that not once in my life have I ever asked myself what I wanted. I've just done what was expected. I honestly don't *know* what I want," she finally concluded after the long silence. "Is that crazy?"

It's not crazy at all. In fact, it's quite common, especially for women. Society demands. Families demand. Work demands. And we're so busy meeting those demands that we don't pause to ask ourselves what we desire.

So ask. Sit with it. And see what comes up.

3. Something big is happening.

Big traumas, messes, and confusion sometimes precede big shifts. It's the classic breakdown before the breakthrough. You, of course, are distracted by the breakdown, not thinking beyond the moment. You can't know where this trauma is leading you. You don't have to. And you shouldn't. You can simply allow it to unfold. Only when it's over will its intention-creating purpose be revealed.

4. You're totally burned out.

Like Rachel, you've been pushing too hard, aiming only at survival and getting by, and you've forgotten who you are. Though Rachel was tempted to dive into a huge overhaul and start over, this was simply her exhaustion talking. What we did together was much more elegant, and not nearly as dramatic. Rachel continued to serve her clients and do the due diligence to get her finances straight. And she gave herself daily quiet space to write in her journal and return to her yoga practice so that she could recover her energy. That's when she began experiencing clarity again and finding enthusiasm for intention. This will happen for you, too. Exhaustion rarely yields a powerful intention.

WHATEVER YOU DO, DON'T TRY TO "FIGURE IT OUT"

Whenever a client uses the words "figure" and "out" in a sentence about intention, I cringe. That's because I know my client is hoping her left brain will rescue her. The left brain, in all of its strategizing, controlling, fixing, and figuring, wants to get its clammy little paws in everything we do.

When I wrote my very first songs, I'd "think them up." I'd have a thought like, *I want to write a song about the Chesapeake Bay Bridge!* Then I'd start "figuring out" how I could write it. Invariably, I'd end up with a boring song that made anyone I played it for smile painfully and say things like, "Well that's nice," when I strummed the last chord.

But then, there was this one night. It was after dinner. I was in my apartment. I was lonely, even empty. I sat down with my guitar on the floor in the skinny little hallway, and I just leaned on the wall and played little fingerpicking patterns.

Before I knew it, a melody showed up. I was tempted to mentally grab it and try to "figure out" where to take that melody. But I didn't. I stayed curious. I didn't push. A lyric here. A melody idea there. I took notes. Still, I worked hard not to "figure it out." Mostly, my job was simply getting out of the way.

That song ended up on my first CD. It was called "Pocketful of Pennies." No, it didn't break out my career. It didn't win a Grammy. This isn't that kind of success story. In fact, it was nothing spectacular, except that it was. It taught me what creativity was really about.

Not just artistic creativity, though. *Any* kind of creation. And intention *is* creation.

LET CURIOSITY LEAD YOU

I've used many solutions to help clients work with and deal with this space of not knowing. "Figuring things out" has never been one of them. Neither has "trying harder." The best way to approach such a state is with curiosity. Here are some ideas to play with if you're hitting a blank with your intention.

If you did know . . .

Sometimes "I don't know" is just our usual knee-jerk response. It's what you've always said the minute you feel the slightest bit confused.

My friend Brooke Castillo, founder of the Life Coach School, teaches a different approach. She asks, "If you *did* know, what would the answer be . . . ?" It's a question meant to unlock the usual brain patterns. And it works wonders, since "I don't know" is sometimes a cover-up for, "I don't believe this is possible."

If money and people's opinions weren't an issue . . .

When "I don't know" stems from a lifetime of listening to other people's opinions or the ever-ubiquitous money fears, let yourself move forward by removing those elements from the equation. This isn't about ignoring reality. We just want to unlock the brain a bit.

If it all just feels too big for you, then get granular.

Some of us are not skilled at *Big Picture* thinking. If this is you, then do yourself a favor and get a little more granular. Break your intention down into doable components.

Start with smaller visions. Think in terms of this week, or just this year. Or even consider the "categories" of your business. What is your intention for products or programs in the coming quarter? Or who do you want to hire? Take some time to reflect on a "digestible" intention as you move into the habit of thinking bigger.

Pay attention to delight.

Years ago, when I was signing CDs after a performance, a woman named Indira got to the front of the line and wouldn't let me sign anything until she shared her story with me.

She opened a manila folder that was tucked under her elbow. She smiled and said, "These are my tax documents from last year. I'm blaming you for something."

No one had ever brought tax documents to one of my shows before, but I laughed and rolled with it.

"I have my own business," Indira said as she pulled out the papers. "And I had to pay more in taxes this year than I've ever paid because I made so much money." She pointed at the impressive revenue number in the box on the form.

"See?" she said, raising her eyebrows.

Holy shit, I thought.

Indira continued happily. "I'm blaming you because I listen to your song 'Right Outta Nowhere' every single morning. That song made me take chances I would never have taken. Which is how I made more money than ever. And I paid more taxes than ever. So it's all your fault."

At this point, we were both laughing. I signed the CDs and said, "Well, Indira, it's great to meet you, my friend. Congratulations to you. You've made my whole night."

And I meant it. My entire being lit up at the thought that I, in some small way, had inspired someone to be bold and take action.

I believe it was that night, years before I ever imagined coaching, that my coaching company started. That delight stayed with me for months afterward. I began paying close attention each time anyone shared similar stories with me about my work inspiring them to take different actions.

So, what delights you? What matters to you? Is it when a client shares a breakthrough with you? Then make sure you aren't in such a rush to "scale" that you lose out on real connections with your clients.

Is it going to learning events and connecting with other business owners? Then work that into your plans.

Is it shooting a quick video on your phone and posting it instantly for your students to enjoy? Then stop worrying about your long-form blog posts that keep you up all night, obsessed by Strunk and White grammar rules.

Take note of what delights you. These delights are bread crumbs. They'll show you the way to the bigger-picture desires that seem out of reach.

As a Soul-Sourced Entrepreneur, awareness, clarity, and setting the intention are your responsibility. They are a part of your everyday routine. In time, they become natural to you, though never really easy. Remember, it's the commitment that creates the confidence, not the other way around.

Your intentions are seeds. Like anything that's planted, the first thing that comes up won't be a beautiful spring-green sprout full of promise. It will be dirt (i.e., your fears, your messed-up behavior patterns, your unsolved mysteries). Dirt isn't a bad thing. Sifting through it and clearing it away is part of the process, part of your expansion. Yet, a lot of people get stuck here, bemoaning the fact of their dirt, instead of doing the work to break through it. The fledgling sprout beneath the surface does not obsess over the fact that dirt exists, and it's going to take *for-freakin'-ever!* to become a flower. It just continues its process. So can you.

With each intention, you define what your business is becoming and who you are becoming. As you move toward your intention, your process will continue, too. Where that process takes you and your business, and how efficiently you get there, will be directly determined by your ability to get clear about your intention and then tap into and manage your power around it.

STICKY-NOTE ENERGY

Kigali International Airport, Rwanda, 9:50 AM

The plane was still boarding. As people filed by her seat, Robbin Jorgensen struggled to answer the question posed by the man sitting next to her. It was a question she got all the time.

Settling in, he'd started asking Robbin the usual things you ask your seatmate: Where was she headed? *Back to the states to deliver a keynote for women CEOs and then to lead a two-day corporate leadership training in Atlanta.* What had she been doing in Rwanda? *Training women entrepreneurs enrolled in a US Embassy program as she laid the groundwork for the economic empowerment center she was building.* Even as she said it, she knew it all sounded epic. Perhaps it was. But when your company's name is Women Igniting Change, that's what you do, right?

And then came the inevitable stumper: "How do you find the energy?"

She didn't know how to answer. She didn't know how she "found" energy. Her life simply seemed to *be* energy.

As she pulled her seat belt tight, Robbin thought of Rwanda and the women she'd worked with all week. As she was saying her goodbyes, one woman, Mutesi, with a baby on her hip, pulled Robbin to her, looked directly into her eyes, and said, "My life is changed. Thank you." Here was her answer. Robbin didn't "find" energy anymore. She didn't have to. Her work now generated it for her.

In some ways, Robbin realized she was a bit like this airplane. The takeoff required the most fuel. But once it got to cruising altitude, it could glide and use wind currents. For Robbin, takeoff had been the hardest part. Her fuel source? Nothing but pure intentions, each one written clearly and concisely on sticky notes. She smiled remembering how sticky notes had covered her house. On mirrors, on the fridge, by her bed. That's where she'd "found" the energy to break through the old thoughts and conditioning that told her big things were for other people, that success in the corporate world didn't mean she could succeed as an entrepreneur, that a divorced mom in her early forties had already missed the chance to start up.

So her first intention had been to leave her corporate job and let go of her six-figure salary. (Sticky note: *I am bold. I am resilient. I am tenacious.*) Once that was done, it was time to build her business. (Sticky note: *I am a wise and kick-ass entrepreneur!*) Then getting corporate clients for her trainings and coaching. (Sticky note: *I work with amazing organizations across the country!*) Then scaling her business. (Sticky note: *I am a $1M business owner with an amazing team.*)

After a while, she stopped needing sticky notes. She was riding the currents. Doors opened almost magically at the merest of her intentions. Just yesterday, she'd met with Rwanda's Minister of Gender. They'd formalized a memorandum of understanding for her Economic Empowerment Center for the women of this country she so adored. She smiled, imagining what her sticky note might've said: *My work changes the hearts, souls, and economic lives of the women in Rwanda!*

MANAGING
POWER

9

POWER REDEFINED

HER: Hold on. You feel sorry for yourself because you're not an alcoholic like me?

ME: I'm just saying you're lucky. *Your* addiction lets you give up the thing you're addicted to. Mine doesn't.

HER: I'm lucky? You're saying I'm *lucky* to be an alcoholic?

ME: I'm saying you're lucky because you can avoid the thing that triggers you, and I can't do that. My thing's food. I can't avoid food.

HER: So you're *jealous* of me because I'm an alcoholic? That's what you're saying?

ME: Well, when you put it that way, it makes me sound addled.

HER: Oh, girl, we're way past addled here.

ME: All I'm saying is that when you're getting over bulimia, cold turkey is not an option. I don't get to remove all the food from my apartment. I can't stop hanging out with friends who eat food or stop going to parties where they serve it. There's no detox period. It's harder than other addictions.

HER: So I was right. You feel sorry for yourself because you're not an alcoholic.

This was an actual conversation that occurred when I was in the beginning stages of healing an addiction that had been relentless and all-consuming for ten years of my life: bulimia.

In my martyred state, I rationalized that other addicts had it easier than me. After all, if you were addicted to cocaine or tequila, you could rid your life of the offending substance. Then you could just show up for your twelve-step meetings and deal with the withdrawals, right?

Never mind the many holes in my logic. The inability to get rid of food felt like an impossible obstacle to my own recovery.

But it turned out to be the exact opposite. This one crushing affliction would become the unlikely access point to my own power. By definition, the process of healing bulimia wouldn't let me play my usual game of sidestepping the thing that caused my problems. I was forced to create an actual relationship with that thing. In this case, food.

I didn't like this. I wanted a quick fix so I could be done with my fucked-up self. I wanted a magic pill that would make it all go away. Or at the very least, a nice, linear, easy-to-follow strategy.

But when someone initiates an intention—whether in life or in business—the manifestation is rarely linear. When I initiated the intention to free myself from the grips of bulimia, no pill appeared, no game plan materialized. "Free," I found out, wasn't something that got scribbled on a handy-dandy prescription pad by a jovial physician. Nor was it the pot of gold at the end of an easy, five-step formula. Free was something I had to *become*.

So I trudged off to appointments with acupuncturists, body workers, and other assorted healers who took me deeper into myself, into this thing called "power." One day at a time, one food choice at a time, one intention at a time, one workout at a time—I learned how to stop fighting myself. I learned how to not "get rid of" anything, but to simply be with myself.

This meant I stumbled my way into and out of binges, emotional triggers, colitis, hating exercise, loving exercise, obsessing on exercise, panic attacks, depression, and whatever mystery symptoms appeared on any given day. I flung myself into my bed dozens of times, thinking, *I'm not capable of this!* or *I'm too sensitive!* or *This is all too much!*

Slowly, though, I began to embrace and embody a new level of energy, of power. The power to make choices and to intentionally create a life. As it turns out, I am the common denominator in all the arenas of my world, which means I have to show up. To be present. So I stopped looking for the escape hatch, and I rebuilt a relationship with food, my body, and my reactions. Three things I could not—try as I might—"get rid of."

THE MECHANICS OF INTENTION AND POWER

When you initiate an intention—whether it's about crossing the million-dollar revenue mark or hiring your first full-time manager—you consciously call something new into your business or your life. You call yourself to *become* the person who can realize that intention. As we discussed in the previous chapter, in its quest to flower, your little seed of an intention is then likely to find itself pushing against a whole lot of dirt—unexpected, uncomfortable, and unrelenting obstacles, some of which are self-inflicted.

Contrary to popular self-help-y beliefs, the appearance of those obstacles doesn't mean you're the one "blocking" the flow, or that you have bad energy, or that you must not want your intention enough. Far from it. If you can learn to recognize, stay with, and work your way through obstacles, you'll engender a whole new level of power: your own power.

Yet few people see it this way. In fact, our culture encourages us to rid ourselves of anything that confronts us. Got pests? Spray the bastards. Got a headache? Four Advil at least. Got weeds? Pound them with a chemical so strong that you wipe out the surrounding ecosystem for at least two square miles. Never mind the side effects. Just carpet-bomb your one specific problem as fast as possible, with as little inconvenience to you as possible.

So it's no wonder most of us don't think to just be with something that's uncertain or challenging. To be curious. To wonder why it's there and what it might have to say. We're trained to get it gone, not to explore our distress or learn from pain. We're not trained in the ways of true power.

Plus, "power" is a weird word. That's an added trigger. It makes us think of evil regimes. Or hateful political agendas. If the idea of accessing or experiencing power makes you feel weary, this might be why. We've turned power into aggression. We've made it about "power *over*." It's the CrossFit Games take on life. Where you don't just succeed. You *crush* it! You don't just have a great day. You beat yesterday! You don't heal bulimia. You make bulimia your bitch! And you don't just get a good night's rest. You kick sleep's ass!

So let me be clear about what I mean by power. For the Soul-Sourced Entrepreneur, power is simply the energy to create things, to transform things, to evolve, to be clear. It's the ability to manage and direct your energy toward an outcome or intention. That's all.

It's "power *to*." Not "power *over*."

And this is why—strange as it sounds—bulimia was my first business mentor. It forced me to see in real time that real power and real solutions come from connection and attention, even in the face of extreme discomfort. Bulimia taught me to stop seeking power over. To stop avoiding uncertainty. To open and be curious instead.

This is right about the point where your typical business type will call me "woo-woo." Or dismiss all of this as a waste of time. Given a choice, most business owners would rather avoid or, yes, crush the many new challenges that accumulate as their business grows. I get it. These reactions come from a lifetime of misunderstanding power.

BEING IN BUSINESS = "BEING IN"

A spa owner named Anita literally acted out this desire in front of the room at her first Uplevel mastermind retreat. She was stressed and edgy. She had heard a hundred business gurus blather on about "outsourcing." But outsourcing wasn't working for her.

As I coached her in a spotlight session, I asked about her team. At one point, she sighed and said, "Look. I just want them to be over there taking care of stuff, while I do my thing over here. That's why I hired them."

I pointed at her. "Don't move!" I said. "Just freeze." I walked up to her. I held her shoulders.

"Anita," I said. "I want you to look where you're facing." Anita's eyes darted around. She nodded, still frozen.

Then I said, "Now, I want you to look at where your business is."

Her back was turned away from the "them" she'd hired. And away from her company.

She was "over here." Her business was "over there." She was waving her hands at "over there," as if it were unrelated to what she was doing "over here." An annoying inconvenience. *Spray the bastards.*

All your life, you may have been told that you're wildly creative. Or you heard over and over about all your potential. Or that you're not a numbers person. Or that with ADHD like yours, you'll have a hard time with details. And, like Anita, you may have heard about this one cool thing that will make your problems go away so you can get back to focusing on all of that potential of yours.

While those descriptions of you may have merit, the thing about owning a business is that you still have to be with your business. Even the tedious parts. We've got a name for this now. We call it "Being In."

I shared this with Anita. I told her that delegating wasn't the same as abdicating. I explained that hiring and training would be tedious for some-one like her. That it meant creating things like criteria and checklists. It meant understanding why certain tasks were even done, how they should be done, and what each looked like when done and done well. And that she'd have to get clear on exactly what experience, skill sets, and tempera-ment the person in each role should have.

In other words, Anita had to stop fighting and avoiding what seemed to overwhelm her. She'd have to navigate and manage her own energy and power.

You will, too.

Sure, there will always be crisis situations when four Advil (or a quick online ad, or a fast firing, or a good tactical email) will do the trick. But more often, there's deeper stuff at the root of the issue. And when you're bold enough not to fight it, but to meet it, see it clearly, remain present, and operate from that place, you'll build an actual fix, master a new skill, or create a true healing so deep that you won't need sprays, gels, liquids, powders, or pills. This is real power. Your power.

10

THE ATTENTION
ECONOMY

P lay a game with me right here.

While you're looking at these words, put your attention on the ceiling. Just keep on reading and place your attention on the ceiling. (I'm even doing this while I write.)

Now, keep reading these words, and place your attention on the wall to the right of you. Hold it there and keep looking at these words.

Now, place your attention on your right ankle. Hold it there. Keep reading.

Now, stop reading. Close your eyes for five seconds, and place your attention into both your hands. I mean, really feel your hands. What is "hand-ness" like for you?

Spooky isn't it?

This is attention. Attention is not just what you happen to be looking at. It's an actual energy.

Your attention is a power you can access, manage, and place at will. As your attention went from spot to spot, most likely you could feel a kind of movement of something as well. Attention gathers the unfixed nature of your overall awareness and focuses it in one place.

Whether it's Anita focusing on the duties of her next hire and making a criteria list, or me preparing a nutritious meal, attention is the currency of our Power To.

In some ways, attention *is* power.

But we're all pretty lame when it comes to how we use, let alone control, our attention. There's a reason I didn't tell you to hold your attention on the ceiling for twenty minutes. You'd be so done with that in seconds, right?

We rarely pause to consider where we place our attention. We're far from being masterful when it comes to holding and directing it. (Though you did just prove you were capable of it.) We let it get jerked around from one bright, shiny object to the next, with no awareness of the impact this has on our outcomes.

As I was healing from bulimia, I discovered I had the power to call my attention back from something that seemed to control me from the time I could say the word "supermodel." I discovered I had the power to stop placing my attention on women's magazines.

This was radical. At least it *felt* radical, hooked as I was by my own story of victimhood. I'd spent my life blaming advertisers, magazines, billboards, and all the images of skinny women everywhere for making me hate my own body. Then it occurred to me that, as the person in charge of placing my attention, I didn't have to give it to these things if I didn't want to.

So I began a new practice. Whenever I was in line at a grocery store or sitting in a waiting room, I'd pull (or yank, or drag) my attention away from the magazines with the perfect cover girls. At friends' houses, I stopped grabbing the fashion magazines that beckoned from coffee tables and bathroom racks. I stopped buying them. I even refrained from glancing at images of women on anything that would hook my mind into its "I should look like that" trance. Now in charge of my attention, I was able to deliberately place it on things that supported my recovery (my intention).

If you've never struggled with addiction, such a minor initial victory might sound pathetic. Or insignificant. But to me, applying this practice felt like I was ripping a huge door, along with its frame, out of a wall and away from a view I'd stared at for years. Then I was reconstructing that doorway to open onto a whole new reality for myself. That's how physical it felt to retrain and reclaim my attention.

Over time, the impact of this one new ability was stunning. I'd extricated myself from the sordid grip of the advertisers. I had taken ownership of my attention and dropped my victimhood story. Nothing pathetic about that.

That's also when I started to understand the connection between attention and the power to manifest an intention.

COMFORTABLE BEING UNCOMFORTABLE

When you "pay attention" to someone or something, you're literally giving—spending, disbursing, investing—a highly valuable resource: your power. Marketers and advertisers have jumped on the phrase "Attention Economy" because in a noisy world, your attention is a scarce commodity, an actual form of tender. In the twenty-first century, the phrase "paying attention" is for real. You are that powerful.

But the players in the Attention Economy are betting on you not understanding that. They're counting on the ease with which you'll hand your attention over to their agendas. And face it. In our case, it's a pretty smart bet. Why? Because when it comes to managing our power and attention, the odds are stacked squarely against us the minute we start a business.

That's because as entrepreneurs, our success is directly correlated to our ability to be uncomfortable. After all, the only way to know if we're on the right road with our intention is to head down that road and into the unknown. To test our pitch. To initiate the fierce conversation. To be a pioneer, uncertain that the destination is even out there. And uncertainty, as we've discussed, is not comfortable. Naturally, our entrepreneur brains are constantly seeking relief, and thus our attention is a cinch to distract.

Think about it. Recall any recent situation when you needed to focus. Say, writing a proposal to a potential client. There you sit, writing. Well, not writing really. But you're at your laptop making a go of it. You know the gist of what you want to say. As usual, you have no idea how to say it. You get all fidgety. And that right there is the first twinge of what seasoned artists call "creative tension," which is just a fancy name for discomfort.

So your thoughts drift. You start to question your sanity and whether or not you even want this stupid client, given all the added work it'll bring. Then you're dreaming of the days when you were an Outward Bound instructor. Man, life was so much simpler then. That's when you look up at the wall and think, *What the hell is* that? On the wall across from your office window, there's a long train of fuzzy lint intertwined with dog hair waving gently in the synchronized gusts of your ceiling fan.

Now you have a choice. You can sit with the discomfort and redirect your attention to the stream of meaningless drivel on that Google doc, as you labor to birth this proposal into the world. Or you can obey the mind when it says, "Well, now, I need to get a damp rag and clean that shit up."

Ladies and gentlemen, here we have some high-octane creative tension.

Powerful people—prolific authors, CEOs, elite athletes, Navy SEALs—train themselves to see this discomfort as part of the process. They expect it. They're prepared for it. And so they don't hand over their attention (and their power) to whatever tempting distraction is waving and shouting "yoo-hoo!" at the mind.

The rest of us, however, aren't aware of or prepared for this brain game. We want nothing more than to shift our attention away from the activity causing the pain and onto something—anything—that might restore calm, order, and a sense of competence.

It's the perfect setup. First, we have a daily situation where, as business owners, in order to succeed, we need to be able to be uncomfortable. Second, we have a mind that doesn't want to feel uncomfortable. Ever. Third, we have a world determined to distract our minds and attention.

My fellow entrepreneurs, creative tension *is* your reality. And these days, wall lint is the least of your problems, which brings us back around to the tender topic of addiction.

INPUT ADDICTION: ATTENTION'S LITTLE METH FIX

I have a theory about addiction. It's always seemed to me that every addiction is about keeping things down.

When you're bulimic, you binge. (Stuff the energy down.)

When you smoke, you inhale. (Suck the energy down.)

When you're an alcoholic, you drink. (Swallow the energy down.)

Yeah, I know—it's more complex than that. But in some ways, compulsive behavior is about stuffing any and all space so full that you avoid the inner experience of discomfort or tension.

So these days maybe you don't grab the Grey Goose or the sleeve of Oreos. (Okay, maybe sometimes the Oreos.) These days, when things get uncomfortable, you give your attention to something much more subtle. More acceptable.

Enter the world of "input."

What's input?

It's thirty-one tabs open in Safari. It's checking how many likes your photo got every seventeen seconds. It's texting, pings, Slack, and an in-box that pokes your desktop every five minutes. Not to mention the latest podcast. (Do I need to keep going here?) The Netflix series you consume (all six of them). And the next book you add to Kindle when you have nine others unread in there. It's bingeing on information just to have information.

In other words, it's anything (content, facts, opinions, data) that will go *in*. Anything that fills up and pushes down whatever is causing discomfort.

Input demands the incessant, knee-jerk activity of "checking." In any moment, we find ourselves facing anything that resembles space—sitting alone at a café, resting between sets of back squats, waiting at a red light—and what's the first thing we do? Reach in our pocket and pull out the phone. We check. See what input might be out there for us. A hit. A snort. An LOL. Some 411. Maybe a disaster. Or even the stupid-ass political thing your brother-in-law just posted.

Whether or not we admit it, that little jolt to ease the tension of being alone with the challenge in front of us, ourselves, or our thoughts, feels good. And people unaware of input's tricks happily hand over their attention—just for a second, then one more, and then another—until distraction takes up (and so makes up) their whole life.

INPUT VERSUS INSIGHT

Ray studied the cars and trucks on I-40 and sighed. A six-hour drive home in this kind of traffic made him more irritated than he already was.

He had just spent two days at a business mastermind working on a single issue. He mapped things out, discussed strategy, formulated plans, and thought—a lot. He'd known going in that he might not get an exact solution to his challenge. Still, he'd hoped he'd at least get something, a little shove in the right direction from all that focus. All he got, however, was frustrated.

Now, at seventy-five miles per hour, Ray searched his phone for a podcast to make him feel better. That's when the horn of the semi jolted him. He snapped his head up, whispered, "Oh crap!" and steered back into his lane. Ray tossed his phone onto the passenger seat where it disappeared into a heap of empty wrappers. Three protein bars, two packs of smoked almonds, and a bulk-foods bag of some kind of cacao-nib trail mix. Technically, he could tell himself it wasn't junk food. But it was evidence of his anxiety. Now, he'd nearly wrecked trying to escape that anxiety.

Rattled by the near miss, Ray did something radical. He grabbed his phone from under the wrappers and switched it off. Totally off. He didn't need GPS. No one had to reach him. His wife was at her mom's with the kids.

He took a deep breath and drove on in silence. He vowed to keep to the right lane and the speed limit, while his thoughts went into overdrive pointing out that other cars were racing around him, that he was bored, that he hated the west side of Knoxville, that maybe he should turn his phone back on and find a podcast. But he kept the phone off and continued his slow, quiet drive.

Eventually the scenery opened up. There were more trees, less city. More green, less gray. As he drove and witnessed and relaxed, an hour passed. Then another. And then something appeared in his awareness. An idea. Just a small thing that slipped in without fanfare. Ray let himself simply play with it to see where it led. In the last hours of his drive, it evolved. It slowly shaped itself into a possible solution to his unfixable challenge.

When Ray pulled into his garage, he ran upstairs to his office computer and typed out his thoughts. He called his business partner and left an excited message. This felt right and real.

Over the coming months, Ray and his partner implemented his idea, and business took off in the direction they'd wanted. Now, Ray looked back on that boring six-hour drive and marveled at the arrival of this aha moment, wondering where it even came from.

Sometimes what breaks our creative tension has nothing at all to do with gathering more information or focusing harder. In fact, a constant flow of input for the sake of more input can clog our brains and stall our creativity. Sometimes our thoughts need space to move around, to find their own connections, and to become what ultimately lands us successfully on the other side of that tension: insight.

Insights are ideas custom-made for your business or life. They're not "answers." They're not even thoughts, really. Insights are little "ahas" or epiphanies. Something previously obscured that's now revealed. Wisdom pointing the way toward how, who, or what's next.

Insights appear when they want to appear and when we're open to them. As such, they can't be forced or pushed or even figured out. We literally must live (and give) into them, experience them. In other words, we must allow the tension to do its work.

In Ray's case, searching for a podcast to occupy his mind was the cherry on top of his input overload that trip. As business owners, our tendency is to left-brain stubborn problems to death, creating mind maps and spreadsheets, or calculating the perfect next steps until we figure it out. At some point, though, our left brain reaches its limits, and all we're doing is obsessively feeding our input addiction.

Sure, left-brain strategic thinking has a place. But it's only one level of power, one type of attention. In musical terms, it's like practicing your scales with a metronome. That's how I started. I played scales—major, minor, pentatonic, you name it—all with the metronome ticking away in the background. It wasn't music. No one listening would say, "Kid, you're gonna be a big star."

Fast-forward a few years. I was on stage. I could play on tempo minus the metronome. I could quiet the strum or pluck a harmonic here and there, and be my own accompanist. The metronomes and scales, the focus and strategizing, were necessary first steps on this journey. But it was only when I emptied my mind and freed my attention that I could make music.

This is part of what Ray experienced. At his mastermind retreat, he was laser focused on his challenge—dissecting it, looking at all angles, and figuring it out. That was the metronome, the scales. The insight came from the space Ray allowed himself outside that structure. The "just driving"— no podcasts, no ruminating, no input. Just quiet, free-roaming attention. His thoughts could marinate. And his unconscious got the time it needed to do its thing behind the scenes.

Unfortunately, our current business world rarely finds the space for insight and intuition—or any kind of subtle perception. It prefers when things are blindingly obvious. Like a good punch in the arm. Or a loud message. Or a consultant who just barks what to do next. Most people don't want space. They don't want to wait. They want an answer. Now.

But insights don't show up and shout answers at us. The only way to get the benefit of insight for your business is to create the free attention it requires.

INPUT DETOX, FREE ATTENTION, AND THE 10×10 BOREDOM BINGE

I'm guessing you're already feeling resistance at the mere suggestion of going without input and the discomfort it might cause. Your brain is most likely already on autopilot, coming up with rational arguments to stave off that discomfort: Free attention is boring. It's a waste of time. It's *nothing*. More information is fun—it's *something*.

But what if you could train yourself to get comfortable being uncomfortable? In my years of working with entrepreneurs and their relentless input addictions, there's a little practice I've created. I call it the 10×10 Boredom Binge because boredom, plain and simple, is what it produces. At least, that's what it feels like at first. This practice helps you get comfortable with discomfort, to detox from your constant need for input, and learn to make room for free attention.

During the 10×10 Boredom Binge, you're not going to meditate. You're not going to pray or write or read. (When it's early days in our input detox, these things, too, can be checked off by our brains as "achievements" of sorts, ranking right up there with input.) Instead, you're going to simply and intentionally get bored and let your mind panic without its usual distractions.

All it takes is three steps and three rules.

Step #1: Take out your calendar.
Step #2: Schedule ten-minute blocks of "Get Bored" time for the next ten days. (And I mean this. Schedule it. Don't just nod your head and say, "Yeah, I should try that.")
Step #3: Show up at the scheduled time. Be bored.

Simple, right? Sure, but it's not easy. So use these three rules of boredom to inform and prepare you.

Rule #1: When we're bored, our usual patterns turn up the volume.

During your ten minutes, expect all kinds of must-dos, must-add-to-Amazon-shopping-carts, must-Google-nows to creep into your mind instantly and with urgency. These are called patterns. Simply say, "Oh! Hello there, pattern!" and notice them.

Also, expect the voice that says, "This is pointless" to make an appearance. That's fine. It's a pattern, too. Each thought will do its damnedest to convince you that it's practical, reasonable, and that following it makes perfect sense. More sense than this stupid boredom thing anyway. Remember that what makes us successful as business owners isn't always what looks the most sensible.

Rule #2: The Boredom Binge is not an "If-This-Then-That" (IFTTT) equation.

IFTTT goes like this: "If I write this code, then my computer will do this." "If I create this filter, then this email will go to this folder." Or "If I sit for ten minutes and be bored—like Christine says—then I will be rolling in the ecstasy of my insights. Like a good Ayahuasca trip."

If that's your expectation, this will suck. Your rational mind will nod along and console you as you bemoan, "This stuff doesn't work." The IFTTT logic is great for programming computers and other feats of engineering. Your personal power, however, is not code. Much of the work you do as a business owner is deeper, more complex, and more mystical than an equation.

Rule #3: This isn't about discipline.

There was one guy I knew in college, who—when I revealed my struggle with eating disorders—told me to "just run more."

Addictions are rarely about the thing you're addicted to. That's just how they manifest. Which is why the 10×10 Boredom Binge isn't about discipline or trying harder. Or giving up social media and phones forever. Why? Because that would last, oh, about three hours.

The Boredom Binge is about practicing something, entering into a relationship with your free attention. Bringing awareness—not judgment—to what you experience and to yourself by noting what you discover. Through repetition, getting comfortable with being uncomfortable, you'll relieve your brain's need for constant input.

THE LOST ART OF CELEBRATION

There's one more thing that sometimes makes us uncomfortable and that we often therefore avoid giving attention to: our achievements. Yet, managing our power well means paying attention to, understanding, and pausing to revel in our success.

For most of us, however, our setbacks claim the majority of our attention by default. If we're not in the middle of a setback, then we're on the lookout for one. Since we want our business to run well, we're incessantly searching for what's not working and focusing our attention on finding some new idea or answer just around the bend. As business owners, we're natural problem solvers and solution finders. Because business *is* problems. (Otherwise, there'd be no need for business, right?)

But being perpetually problem-focused keeps us reaching, striving, and attuned to only the negative. After a while, all that negative attention turns into one massive struggle habit.

Giving attention to positive achievements unwinds that momentum. Celebrating when something goes right freezes the moment. It puts a pin in it. It ensures we acknowledge our wins and recognize the effort it took to achieve them. It also brings our expanded abilities to our attention, giving us confidence in who we are becoming, so we feel ready to take on the next task in our expansion.

Consider how my dog became a champion at catching food in midair:

My husband and I sat on the sofa with a bowl of popcorn.

Our dog sat in front of us, her big brown eyes staring intently.

We began flinging.

Piece by piece we tossed popcorn at her.

At first, she watched each kernel fly by. She became the ball girl at a tennis match, running after each one, picking it up. She'd look frantically at us again as we pelted her with more popcorn. She was utterly confused as kernels bounced off her face.

After about thirty-seven misses, she opened her mouth.

And she caught one.

For a brief moment, everything stopped. The three of us just looked at each other dumbfounded. My husband and I were shocked. So, it seemed, was our dog.

We jumped up as if she'd scored the winning run. We shouted, "Good girl! Good girl!" We pumped our fists. We patted her excitedly. It was our own living room version of the 1951 radio baseball moment: "The Giants win the pennant! The Giants win the pennant!"

After that, with the exception of raw broccoli, my dog caught any food you tossed her way.

Okay, I know. You're not a dog. (Though you could do much worse than being *my* dog.) But when it comes to your business, regularly and purposefully focusing your attention on, acknowledging, and celebrating achievement is key to creating momentum and growth. It's something we all desperately need when it comes to managing our power.

Sadly, most of us get lost in thoughts like, *Thirty-seven kernels of popcorn and I haven't caught a single one!*

If you always set the bar just above your head, as most of us do, then you'll always feel like you're reaching, like you haven't accomplished a single thing. That gets exhausting and defeating. And before you know it, you're looking for some kind of distraction to get you out of this rut.

By making a practice of celebrating even the smallest accomplishment, you stay aware of what you have done and can do. You create energy to spare, and that builds power reserves. Best of all, it feels good, and it's not that hard. Think of it as a daily attentionizer.

You've probably heard of gratitude journals, and you've probably even done one—or continue to do one. Their impact is cumulative. By regularly capturing the things you're grateful for, you naturally notice even more things in your life worthy of your gratitude.

Well, we're going to do something similar here. But our gratitude is going to be for our accomplishments, the gains we make each day, however large or small.

So get a notebook or your phone or computer (I do this digitally), anything that can keep a log. At the end of every day for the next thirty days (or more) write down three things you want to celebrate yourself for doing, not doing, dealing with, focusing on, or whatever. Then pause, reflect on, and celebrate each. Share them with your partner or spouse. Send them via text to a friend.

This little practice will train your attention in the direction of joy and celebration for what has gone right, creating a reservoir of power for you.

Your attention is sort of like the conveyor belt that channels your power. You're in charge of where it's placed. Sometimes you'll need to focus it on one challenge or task. Sometimes you'll need to set it free. Just remember that where you place your attention literally defines the moments your life is made of. Be careless with it and your life is filled with pointless distractions and things that are important to others. Place it purposefully—with clarity and awareness—and it can bring your intention to reality.

DEAR MOMMY, I HOPE SOMEDAY YOU HAVE A DAY OFF

The W Hotel, Atlanta, Georgia, 3:25 PM

A giant bar of dark chocolate was torn open on the table, beckoning me. At the break, I chose to exploit my role as the event leader, hopping off the stage to sidle up to a graphic designer named Michelle. I asked her to help a sister out with a few squares of chocolate.

Michelle laughed, pushed the bar my way, and seized the opportunity, hitting me with a question: "How does someone end these cycles of feast or famine in their business?"

It's a great question. It's *the* question of the solo business owner. And I had to figure out a way to answer in the time it takes to eat three squares of chocolate. (Okay, five.)

Michelle had all the telltale signs of artist turned entrepreneur. Her design work was top-notch, but it kept her working nights and weekends, as her roster of demanding clients texted and phoned at all hours. Her husband, a lifetime bureaucrat, was hesitant to encourage Michelle in what he saw as a risky venture. His responses to her struggles often involved nostalgia for the days when she worked at an ad agency and got a steady paycheck.

Michelle knew she needed to make more money, but that only conjured up images of more time being siphoned away, which made her want to cry. Especially since the prior week her eight-year-old daughter Harper, introverted and artistic just like Michelle, had affixed a Post-it Note onto Michelle's computer that said: "Dear Mommy, I hope someday you will have a day off. Love, Harper." Tears spilled from Michelle's eyes as she shared this with me.

I stopped eating and stared at Michelle. "How serious are you about this question of yours?" I asked.

She stared back. "Hardcore."

"Okay then. You'll need to be relentless. About your emotions. About your patterns. And about shifting them. Approach this like you're training to be an Olympic athlete."

An almost imperceptible wave of fear swept over Michelle's face, but it swiftly vanished. She was in. For too long now, she had played small, dreaming of having confidence in this thing she only sometimes called a business.

Just one year later, Michelle had turned it around. She had doubled her income. She no longer worked on weekends. She turned off the computer at 6 PM every day. And she single-handedly paid for the family vacation using profits from her business.

These days, Michelle has clients who pay her $30,000 for her VIP-level package. She no longer calls herself "just a graphic designer." She's now an in-demand brand stylist. (Her husband is begrudgingly impressed.)

Did she turn into a hard-ass? Did she learn Reiki and clear

out every last bit of dark energy? Did she "heal her inner artist?" No to all of these.

What Michelle did was continually ask laser-like questions about her energy. She paid close daily attention every single time her power got drained. She meticulously noted when she made choices or took actions that dishonored her business. She stopped engaging with people and things that drained her energy and wasted her time. She stopped shrinking.

Working at the living room table? Not gonna happen. She cleared out the upstairs bedroom and made a beautiful office, taking advantage of the dappled light from the trees. Clients who texted at eight o'clock at night when she was reading to Harper? Nope. She set clear boundaries, letting go of anyone who didn't honor them. Holding on to that one draining client because he was her main source of income? Hell to the no. It was terrifying, but she let him go several months after she established a new premium pricing structure.

Michelle learned to match her energy to her intentions. She started to feel and act like an owner, a Soul-Sourced Entrepreneur.

Yes, it had been uncomfortable. But it was so worth it when the agency she used to work for called to inquire about becoming her client. And now people in her life regularly comment, "You're more confident these days." "What are you doing differently?" "Can I do it, too?" To that last question, Michelle thinks to herself, *If you're serious. If you're* all in. *Then, yes, you can.*

11

ENERGY DOESN'T LIE

Years ago, my life was forever changed by some used furniture and a mentor who was wise enough to spot an obstacle I didn't even know was there.

Despite my meticulous focus on where I placed my attention, there were areas in my business where I kept falling into ruts and spinning my wheels. When my mentor suggested we "hop on the phone," I figured he was going to help me sort out my latest mess. But he didn't help me sort. He didn't feel sorry for me. All he did was give me an assignment.

"Christine, deal with your basement."

Since we'd started working together, he'd listened to me complain about the vast amount of crap that had accumulated in the five hundred square feet below my living space. Every time I went down there, I got overwhelmed and headed right back upstairs.

Still, I was miffed. And scared. "Why this? Why now?" I asked. "And what did this have to do with anything?" I wanted someone to fix my business problems, not send me on a declutter mission.

He didn't answer my questions, and he ignored my petulance and fear. He simply broke down the assignment for me.

Thirty minutes a day. One section at a time. Build momentum as you go. And no phone calls with him unless I had concrete progress to report.

It began with old clothes. As I went through the first pile, I came up against a barrage of beliefs that said if I paid too much for it, I had to keep it as punishment. Then, those same thoughts turned right around and said that if I got it on sale, I had to keep it because it was such a bargain. And still others that said if I didn't fit into it anymore, I was to keep that item as a reminder of the days when I apparently had more self-control.

For me, holding on was a form of punishment. Hiding it all in my basement didn't make the punishment any less real. I had all kinds of charge around money, paying too much, making mistakes, and of course, my weight.

I shared this with my mentor, stunned that I had so much baggage around my baggage. With his encouragement, I ceremoniously packed things up, took them to Goodwill, and began to loosen the stronghold of judgment, low self-worth, and general insanity. Instantly, I noticed a higher level of energy in daily activities. A few unexpected opportunities came along.

Then I hit a wall.

I had made my way around to the part of the basement where various pieces of furniture were piled, looking solemn and heavy and dark. A bookcase, a table, a dresser, some shelves, a chair.

When I moved to Asheville, all of my belongings fit in the back of my car. So when I found my first apartment, I went to flea markets and yard sales to furnish the place.

A few years later, when my music was supporting me, I chose to decorate the house I now owned only with items I loved. So one by one, down to the basement each of these old pieces of furniture went. My surroundings became more about beauty and less about budget.

Oddly, I didn't get rid of the stuff. I just stashed it in the basement.

My mentor was curious about this choice. On the phone he asked me, "So, why not just let these things go?"

When I'm asked a simple question like this, sometimes my only answer is "I don't know." Because I don't. But this time I knew immediately. This wasn't a mystery. It was just embarrassing. I told him anyway.

"I think something in me believes that if my music career doesn't work out, I might need these things one day. If I fail, and I don't have any money, I might wish I'd kept them."

Long pause.

"So, you'll be on the street—but at least you'll have that bookcase?" he said.

Okay, point taken. But still, rational thought—even when laced with a bit of smart-assedness—isn't always a catalyst for action.

So what my wise mentor said next has become a critical lesson in power and the actions required to manage it. "Everything in our lives has energy. Everything vibrates, so to speak. And you can believe to your very core that you're vibrating all the right ways with all your positive thoughts. But energy doesn't lie. When we're not congruent, a chaotic vibration operates in the background of our lives. On the surface, we say we want something. But underneath, our energy is actually living out the exact opposite of that thing. Old furniture is no exception."

In essence, I was unconsciously giving more power to that bookcase than to my intention. While I may have been affirming all kinds of success and big outcomes, the vibration coming from my basement was telling the truth. What it was saying to the Universe (and ultimately to me) was this: I believe so deeply in my own failure that I'm holding on to physical things that represent that possibility. Every time I walk by these items in my basement, I'll be reminded of my inevitable downturn. Every moment I'm in my house, my entire being will know that in the very foundation of my life (my basement), there are items that prove I don't believe in my success. I may say all kinds of positive things, but my spirit is draining out of me to these items. My affirmations, in essence, are lies.

The very next morning, I called Habitat for Humanity.

I'd love to report that I smiled and waved as the clunky furniture was loaded onto that truck and carried away. But what I experienced could best be described as terror. It felt like something was being ripped out of me. And it was. I was giving up my Plan B. I was essentially letting my actions proclaim: "I thoroughly trust in my power and believe in my success. How about them apples, Universe?"

This was my own firewalk, raw and barefoot. I had never been so bold.

I was never ballsy in my life, ever. I just wasn't wired with or taught this level of confidence.

But I finally got it.

CONGRUENCE: THE BACKSTAGE OF YOUR BUSINESS

After that experience, I began a relentless analysis of my business activities to see where I was placing my energy and where I wasn't congruent. I paid close attention to my internal reactions to and the "vibration" from everyone and everything. I called it my Business Backstage. No matter how shiny and cool I looked on the front stage at my performances, the energy operating in the backstage would always tell the real truth and create the real results.

I started asking myself some deep, searching questions.

When did I say yes just so I would get the approval I thought I needed?

How did I avoid a situation rather than face the truth it was revealing?

Where did I spend money on things I didn't want as a cheap substitute for something I did want?

When did I waste more time trying to get something for free, rather than investing in myself?

Most of my power problems could be sourced back to three key areas: people, time, and things.

1. People

From photographers I hired to producers I collaborated with, my relationships were often formed by default. They just sort of happened to me. I didn't reach out to people I wanted to work with. I didn't consider whose talents were best suited for my intentions or the emotional attitudes of the person I'd be paying to support my work.

In my "struggling artist" narrative, I based major decisions on who was cheapest or who maybe happened to be there. So—surprise, surprise—I often ended up working with someone who wasn't up to the task or a good fit for my vision. The situations either drained my energy outright or caused a slow, steady leak.

2. Time

As entrepreneurs, time is part of our economy. Up until this point, I didn't treat my time as valuable. I let myself get pulled in all directions, thinking I could and should do everything. So nothing in my business ever got the time it deserved or needed.

Acting as my own assistant, for instance, I got caught up in menial tasks like deleting names from my mailing list, collating mailers, and sending out emails—hours that could've been devoted to honing my songs and performance.

Worse, I was a bad assistant. I took unsubscribes personally and floundered when anything felt like criticism. I got lost in details, emotions, and minutia. This is part of the deal when you're first getting started, but my incompetence in this area was now eating up days. I gave far more energy to my fear of paying someone than to honoring myself as a budding master of my craft.

3. Things

Then there were my environments. After the furniture experience, "stuff" stopped being just stuff. My surroundings took on new relevance.

I noticed that my so-called frugality often cost me professionally and stole my sense of worth. I'd stay at the cheapest motels when I was on the road, assuming that "this is what musicians do." But navigating a one-star motel room—complete with a shitty mattress, bad lighting, and an all-night sex extravaganza on the other side of the paper-thin wall—was a complete drain.

I never linked the impact of these environments to the quality of my performances. I expected myself to crawl out of these dark holes and shine bright for my audience. Quite the tall order.

I created a name for these misalignments as I spotted them. I called them "incongruencies." I made a regular practice of examining every aspect of my Business Backstage to ensure it operated on the same plane, if not a higher one, than my front stage.

I became selective about who I allowed into my world. I hired an assistant. I got intentional about my environment. And almost effortlessly, offers rolled in for better shows with better pay.

Interesting.

BUSINESS BACKSTAGE: YOUR ENERGY INVENTORY

No matter how hard you work or how much you "hustle," all that drive and effort is no match for the power of your incongruencies. In the end, your backstage always wins. In some ways, hustle and struggle can seem like easier strategies than straightening out your mess backstage. You're used to them. And hey, all the cool kids are doing it.

Entering and dealing with your Business Backstage forces you to face the truth of your own energy and power. You discover how you've avoided, ignored, chosen, or allowed what's there. This is why so many fall back on good old-fashioned busy-ness. It's not as daunting. Not as stark. Not as lonely. But it also keeps you stuck in a chaotic vibration. Facing the truth and investing the time and attention to own what you've avoided, ignored, and allowed transforms you, so you can move on.

If you've initiated a game-changing intention, then your next step is to take an inventory of your backstage. Explore where your power is getting drained and investigate the following questions.

People

1. Among my employees and contracted support is there anyone who is not up for the task or who is draining me or my time? What exactly keeps me holding on to these people? What kind of person would be ideal in this role?
2. Is there any service provider or vendor who's no longer the right person to work with? Again, why am I holding on to them? And what qualities would an ideal vendor have?
3. Among friends and others I spend time with, are there any relationships that are no longer supportive? Where am I tolerating or dealing with behaviors or actions that drain me on a regular basis?

Time

1. What are five things I love to do in my business/work that also bring in income and support the business?
2. What are five things I resist or even despise doing that drain my energy but that need to get done? Do I have to be the one who does them?
3. If I'm being honest, what habits or activities do I spend time on mindlessly, simply because I've always done them? (An example might be looking through email before beginning work.) Is this something I need to be doing? If so, is there a more mindful, more productive way to approach it?

Things

1. True or false: My environment supports my best self. The spaces where I work, relax, and play are exactly how I want them—free of clutter, piles, and other messes.

2. If the answer is false, what needs to change?
3. In my efforts to be frugal, where might I be shortchanging my business success? Broken, outdated, or damaged equipment? Cheap supplies?

This inventory is not a slash-and-burn mission. For instance, when you discover people in your life who are draining you, there's no need to rush to "get rid of" them. For now, start with awareness. You're the one who created all this, either by design or default. Now that you're observing more clearly, give those observations time to sink in. Give your energy the time to shift, so you can make different choices. Sometimes the awareness alone is enough to bring about changes without having to force anything.

To download a supremely cool printable copy of the Energy Inventory and other tools in this book, visit www.SoulSourcedBook.com.

CONGRUENCE AND MONEY

If you're thinking that "people, time, and things" could just as easily be labeled "money, money, and money," you'd have a point. After all, if you didn't hire the best person for the job, it's most likely because the best person charged too much. Or if you decided on the motel room that smelled like a frat house, it's probably because you couldn't justify plunking down an extra fifty bucks for a better one. Or if you wasted four hours last week futzing with the printer, and driving back and forth to the big-box store after buying the wrong toner, I'd guess it's because you refuse to pay for a freakin' assistant!

I get it. I can still remember the exact city in Minnesota (and the eighteen inches of snow on the ground) where I had three nights off on a tour and opted to invest a whole $150 a night for a nice hotel room. Visions of future me standing in food-stamp lines and pushing shopping carts down the middle of cold city streets haunted me as I handed over my credit card.

I stuck with my decision and aligned with my intention. And guess what? While I was staying in these spacious digs, I was able to work, write songs, and focus on my upcoming schedule. On one of those days, I got three performance contracts that totaled thousands. Coincidence? I've learned to think not.

When it comes to money and power, there are two camps out there.

First, there's the "suck it up" camp. These are the folks who say that no matter what, you never spend more than you make because debt is evil. Use your time getting as much stuff as you can for free or cheap. Budget everything to the last penny.

The other camp is the "abundance mindset" people. These folks say that if you go out and buy yourself those Jimmy Choos, your dreams of stepping on stage as a national speaker will manifest because your intention is so strong now that you have the shoes.

Neither is right. Neither is wrong. There's wisdom in both camps.

The Soul-Sourced Entrepreneur, however, operates in a zone outside of these well-worn rules and concepts. Money is no longer just about that one number. To the Soul-Sourced Entrepreneur, money is a channel for our energy. And to operate at our highest level, we know that our energy must align with our intention. So we look at the energy of money through the filter of two verbs: spend and invest.

Consider Josh. Josh is a personal trainer who works at the local gym. He fantasizes about starting his own business and sometimes shares his big plans with me, asking for my input.

In one conversation, he learned that I had a subscription to an elite online fitness site. He asked for my log in and password. He already had access to a few other sites like this from his friends, but this site was different. It was created by his idol, a trainer who has coached Olympians and world-class athletes.

Now, here's how the mind thinks: Christine has more money than I do. I have big dreams. If Christine gives me the log in to a site that might help me, it's no skin off her back. And I get to see what my idol does to be so successful!

Makes logical sense, right? On some level, yes. But let's consider congruence.

If Josh opens his own business as a personal trainer, he'll be asking people to invest in themselves, in their health, and in their wellness. Your average person doesn't want to part with their money because that's what they think they're doing—parting with it, spending it. Sure they'll do it if "the company pays for it" or "it's covered by insurance." Otherwise, they see Josh's fee as *spending*.

They've never considered the other verb here: invest.

Investing leads to a return. Maybe that return isn't immediately in the form of the money. Maybe it's better health. Maybe it's more confidence. This might mean making more money in a backdoor kind of way—like you invest in your health and you're no longer embarrassed to go out for job interviews because you love how you look. But that's hard to predict at first. And it takes some time and experience to see how money pays off in non-money ways. You have to do it to find out.

By asking for my log in, Josh was living his life from the "spend" model. He didn't want to spend money on his business and personal growth to build his ultimate financial and soulful success. He wanted to get that for free.

And there's the "incongruency."

The minute Josh starts a business, he'll be asking people to step into the invest model by working with him. All the sales tactics in the world won't help him if he has never himself invested in his own growth. He won't have experience in how returns on personal investments work. And he won't—because he can't—empathize with the fear and doubt potential clients struggle with when they're on the verge of investing in themselves. (Also known as the sales conversation.) At best, he'll be convincing people. He'll see it only as getting a sale or not getting a sale.

Years ago, I hosted a training online about money and entrepreneurship. In that training, I talked about Josh. Somewhere in Brooklyn, New York, a computer programmer named Khaiim was watching. His heart started racing.

Holy shit, he thought. *I'm that trainer dude.*

Khaiim was struggling. A rapper and hip-hop poet, his intention was to quit his day job and inspire audiences full-time with his words and music. He was powerful on the stage—and great at his craft. But he wasn't getting the gigs. And the ones he got paid him close to nothing.

Khaiim sat back in his chair. *My whole message is about abundance and believing in your power,* he thought. *But damn, I don't live that way.*

Khaiim had every reason to not live that way. He grew up in the streets. He was a smart kid and quickly learned how to use his smarts to cut corners, get things for free, and dodge extra costs at every turn. It was survival.

When his computer programming skills got noticed and netted him a paying job, he could afford rent. Then, a mortgage. But the cutting-corners behavior had become a part of who he was. As a hacker, he could make his way into anything. It wasn't stealing, was it? It was hacking. So he accumulated access to many trainings and programs to collect all the information and education he wanted—about art, music, entrepreneurship, and productivity.

Suddenly Khaiim saw the disconnect between his performance and his life. Sure, he was rapping about positivity and thriving, but he operated every aspect of his business as if he was still just surviving. He was asking promoters to invest in his message, while he was getting other people's messages for free and with a scarcity mindset.

That night, in the blue glow of his desktop, Khaiim went through his files one by one and cleared out every single free and hacked program and training. Over the coming months, he cleaned up other areas of his life as well.

After that, he chose to invest in an Uplevel mastermind. Energized by making a financial commitment, he showed up fully. Using what he was learning, he changed his entire pricing structure. He created tiered performance "packages." He set his fees to reflect the value. He created systems for attracting ideal clients and promoters, and for how people hired him.

So was he surprised when he started asking for—and getting—$10,000 for premium performance dates? Was his wife surprised when he started to pay the mortgage—as promised—month after month? At first, yes. But now that he's quit his programming job and makes his living from his music (and still paying the mortgage), Khaiim has a different perspective.

"I realized that if I wanted to be credible to my audiences, I had to live my words," Khaiim said. "If I wanted people to commit their time, energy, and money to improving themselves, I had to commit my time, energy, and money to improving myself. Whatever I wanted to receive, I had to give."

That's congruence.

Your business is the territory of your soul's expansion. Money is one of the forces that contributes to that expansion. That's because when you own a business, you are on the line for every single last thing. And you must name the value and worth of every single last thing. The corporation doesn't write your check. You do.

No one gives you a title that conveniently dictates your worth. You choose that.

No one can place you in a hierarchy that reveals your value. You determine that.

As Khaiim discovered, this is huge work. It'll bring you face-to-face with old rules or excuses or maybe even slippery shortcuts you've felt justified taking. But energy doesn't lie. And congruence is much bigger and deeper than being a "good" or "bad" person. It's about aligning with your intention. Your business can be a great teacher for those vital lessons to become your personal victories.

DESERVITUDE

People do funny things with ideas like congruence. The ego might read all of this, for instance, and turn it into an excuse to go out and just buy shit. And before you know it, "invest in yourself" becomes a Tesla, a high-rent luxury office space, and a fancy new wardrobe item with a label that says "Prada." After all—the logic goes—that's congruent with me being a "badass entrepreneur!"

Which is exactly *not* what I'm saying. That's just your ego conflating the idea of "congruence" with the idea of "deserving" so it can avoid the discomfort of doing the real work.

A word like "deserve" carries with it the energies and attitudes designed to cover up the fear of not knowing, or shame for not having "arrived" yet, or the raw ache of your own vulnerability. (An unwelcome trait in business.) So a false self is created and justified. Your power is siphoned off to support the justification. And your vibration becomes chaotic—bouncing between what your business needs to better align itself and what your ego needs to stroke itself.

12

POWER PLAYS: THE INNER GAME OF BUSINESS

When Asheville songwriter David Wilcox was at the peak of his mainstream commercial success, I was a few months into gigging regularly at local bars.

One afternoon, when David was between road trips on a rare stint home, I told him about a disturbing trend at my gigs. Whenever I played cover tunes—Janis Joplin, the Eagles, Sheryl Crow—everyone would whoop, cheer, scream, and stuff cash into my tip jar.

Then I'd perform my own tunes. And crickets.

I whined that I was wasting time writing my own stuff. With my head in my hands, I looked up at David and said, "I like it better when they clap."

"Okay," he laughed. "But that right there—that little need for applause—is how some really brilliant artists end up as cover acts when their big dream was to make their own music. They give their power over to the instant hit of praise. They let the high of applause in the moment determine their career path."

I instantly felt what he meant. I could see my ego getting all puffed up when people whooped in drunken elation for "Peaceful Easy Feeling." And I could feel how, when someone left the bar in the middle of one of my original tunes, a bit of my life force walked out with them. Goodbye soul. Hello "Margaritaville."

"If you can play your songs and live through that emptiness, you'll grow your following," David continued. "The people who stay, the ones who listen, will become your fans. It won't be many at first. But it'll build. Your job right now is to pull your power back from the quick hit of easy applause. They're clapping because they know the song. Not because of you. Be you. It's not about the applause."

I carried David's words with me like a charm in my pocket. I saw my power fling itself at the people mumbling and laughing at the bar after the last strum of one of my songs. At people who clapped half-heartedly, never looking up from their table conversations. Or at a promoter who said, "Not interested."

Over time, I became acutely attuned to the empty feeling that came along with handing my power (and my intention with it) over to someone else, their opinion, their demand, or even to what I thought *might* be their opinion or demand.

Then I used that awareness. I became an alchemist. Instead of seeing myself as defective, I learned to see this as a pattern that could be triggered, which is how I learned to call my power back to me.

HOW POWER GETS LOST—AND FOUND

Margaret had initiated her intention for the year—to make $125,000 in business revenue, twice what she'd ever made. She was fired up. But it meant raising her prices, which made her feel sick. She dreaded rejection. Still, she stood in the power of her intention and made the changes.

At least on paper.

Less than a week later, she came face-to-face with her first opportunity to take her new rates for a spin. A local business reached out and set up a "get-acquainted" call with Margaret. On the call, she went through her sales process. She created a relationship with the CEO. He was excited. Then the big moment came. She walked through the features and benefits of her services, showing him how her customized operating systems would save time and remove frustration for him and his whole team. Then, she revealed her new pricing structure.

Silence.

Margaret knew she should allow the silence (the tension) to be there. But after what seemed like forever, she couldn't handle it. Before she knew it, she heard herself say, "Or, I could always just . . ." Then she heard herself offer a discount. A big one, which, of course, he jumped on.

Margaret's trigger was silence. It started a wave of fear. Fear of judgment. Fear of loss. Ultimately, the fear determined her fee. Not her. Not her intention.

When Margaret hung up the phone, instead of being excited about a new client, she was depressed. Yet again, she'd be doing too many hours of work for too little money.

When we unconsciously hand our power over to someone or some circumstance, we're usually trying to avoid pain or discomfort. "Please be my client! I'll lower my prices. Will you approve of me then?" And that's when we step out of alignment with our intention and get lost in an old power-draining pattern.

But we can use our intention to retrieve our power. It starts with awareness—calling to mind our intention and then honestly weighing whether or not our actions (or reactions) align with our intention. Awareness allows us to reclaim the moment and choose an intention-congruent response.

Once Margaret consciously recognized phone silence as the trigger that caused her to hand over her power, she got strategic. She planned in advance how she could be present during that pain. She even scripted answers to typical objections and practiced them. She also decided that her new win would be to allow the silence. This helped her not obsess about getting the sale.

A few weeks later, she was on another get-acquainted call. She explained how she worked and stated her fees. Then she stopped talking.

The inevitable silence came. Along with her inevitable self-deprecating thoughts: *I'm overpriced. I'm a fraud and he knows it. He hates me.* The tension was almost unbearable. But this time, she stayed with it. She remembered her intention and that silence was not the enemy.

When the prospect finally spoke, he said, "I'll be honest with you, that's much more than I thought it'd be. Do you have anything cheaper?"

At this point, Margaret wanted to say, *Cheaper? Of course I have something cheaper! Are you kidding me? How about free? Would that work?* She saw herself reaching through the phone and wrapping her arms around this man's ankles, begging him not to reject her.

She took a deep breath. As she'd rehearsed in her head, she asked her inner drama queen to chill out for a bit. Finally, when she was ready, she recited her script: "I agree with you, I am priced at a premium. But that's because I provide such a high level of service. So no, I don't offer cheaper packages." Miracle of miracles, she didn't apologize.

More painful silence. She breathed, just like she'd practiced.

After what seemed like forever, he said, "Okay. Let's do it. I want to make this happen!"

This time, Margaret hung up the phone elated. Not because of the new client. And not because of the money—almost triple her old prices. But because she'd gotten her big win. She lived through the silence. She'd experienced her ability to break through a power-deflating pattern that had operated in the background since she started this business.

These are the big victories. We've been conditioned to believe that as entrepreneurs, we should all be bungee jumping out of our fears or patterns. Or busting through a finish line with confetti raining down and raucous cheering.

But calling our power back is often a deeply silent experience. Margaret didn't head butt anyone as she shifted this pattern. Neither did I as I performed my own tunes to distracted bar audiences. This stuff is uncomfortable and deep. But in the end, discounting her fees wouldn't make people value Margaret. And playing "Freebird" wouldn't make anyone love me.

So we build a practice out of spotting our power drains, taking charge of our actions, and calling our power back to us.

THE PATTERN RECOGNITION AND RE-SCRIPTER TOOL

This is what I call an awareness tool. It's a way to identify your recurring power drains and then set up a course of action to manage them in advance, reclaiming and redirecting your power. You might not be perfect at this at first. Like Margaret, you may wrestle through the re-script. But this awareness alone will begin to shift the usual pattern.

Step #1: Identify recurring triggers.

Consider your business right now. Make a list of five situations in the last month that elicited an emotional reaction from you.
Examples:

A client gave negative feedback about your team's work.
A social media post made you feel left out of the action.
An email contained an invitation to a function you didn't want to attend.
A prospect said no.
Your proposal was rejected and a competitor got the job.

Step #2: Choose one of your triggers and list three to five thoughts that arise when it occurs.

Remember, you're seeking awareness here. Not indulgence. You don't need to relive the scenario. Just be curious and write down the thoughts that first come up.

For instance, a competitor getting a job for which you were rejected might cause thoughts such as:

"I'll never be successful. I'll always struggle."
"What a waste of time. I need to stop doing proposals."
"They think I suck."
"My dad was right. I'm not business minded."

Step #3: Describe the behaviors or actions these thoughts propel.

Be specific. For example:

I call my sister for sympathy.
I do things with an air of resentment for the rest of the day. And then I'm mean to my kids and spouse at dinner.
I shut down. I tell myself I deserve a break. And then I don't work much at all for three days. But I don't relax either.
I avoid phone calls and emails from anyone because I feel so humiliated.

Step #4: Create an Instant-Response Action Plan.

What? We're not going to try to change the horrible thoughts?

No, we're not.

Sure, we could reframe this situation. And you may do that eventually. But fighting thoughts is a losing battle, especially when you're lost in a pattern. Patterns are deeper than thoughts. Instead, let's create an environment where these triggered thoughts don't get fertile ground to thrive and determine your behaviors.

For instance, as much as Margaret wanted to, she knew she couldn't stop or change her post-offer, mid-silence thoughts. They ran too deep. But by writing up instructions for how to behave during the silence, she could ensure those thoughts didn't determine her behavior, even as they raged.

The reality is that most of us don't have control over the thoughts that come into our heads. So fighting them usually ends in a battle of thoughts. We can prevent all that by scripting out a few simple steps for keeping our behavior aligned with our intention, no matter what pops into our heads.

Examples:

"I allow the silence and breathe, even as my thoughts try to convince me they are true."
"I take a ten-minute walk without podcasts or music to distract me."
"I stay with myself and let the feelings rush through me without reacting to them."

Bonus Step: Define a New Win.

Instead of forcing yourself to make every situation a do-or-die result, make your goal your win, make breaking the pattern itself your measure of success—just as Margaret did. As long as she can sit through the silence without offering a knee-jerk discount, Margaret now calls it a win, and she celebrates, sale or no sale.

I used this process when I was preparing to record my third CD. I wanted to work with a new producer. Up until this point, I'd only worked with whoever was local and convenient. On this record, however, I wanted to experiment, to push myself and my art. But I had no manager to create any kind of excitement or buzz to inspire a talented producer to work with me. More to the point, I had no one to do the asking for me. If I wanted a quality producer, it was up to me to get one.

So I made a list of my six favorite record producers in no particular order. And then I paused to reflect on what could derail me. What was my biggest trigger?

Well, obviously it was rejection. It was someone saying "no."

As per my usual pattern at the time, I made "no" mean that I wasn't good enough, and that this person's opinion was the truth. Which would lead to some form of giving up. If that happened on the first attempt, it would mean not expanding or reaching out to anyone else. It would mean going backward and settling.

So I scripted out my action steps in the face of a negative response.

Step #1: Sit quietly and breathe for three to five minutes.
Step #2: Pull out my list of producers and see whose name is next.
Step #3: Contact that producer using the script I'd written in advance.
Step #4: Send music samples.
Step #5: Follow up in five days if there is no response.

In other words, I taught myself to say, "What's next?" I also taught myself to get good at rejection. In fact, my ultimate victory was taking the next action in the face of my sensitivity (a victory I recognize even to this day). In the end, I worked with the perfect producer and discovered that finding the right people is more about a good match than whether my music, my company, or my work is good enough.

Letting your triggers have your power and determine your behavior is how you allow the same old stories to determine the fate of your business. When I didn't give my reactions or emotions any chance to create my behaviors, it was a breakthrough of epic proportions. No head butts or high-fives required. It just felt awesome.

To download a supremely cool printable copy of the Pattern Recognition Tool and other tools in this book, visit www.SoulSourcedBook.com.

THE UNEXPECTED POWER OUTAGE

Even when you've experienced that elated internal victory of breaking through old power drains and patterns, it doesn't mean you won't get blindsided sometimes. The nature of energy and power is subtle. It goes way beyond thinking positive, having the perfect affirmative thoughts, and relentlessly going for it. Power and its patterns are a constant movement. Which means, even when you've conquered some deeply embedded power drains, you can get triggered in any moment and not even spot the hit until several nights later, when it's 2 AM and you find yourself barefoot in your kitchen next to an empty Cheesecake Factory box, wearing only a nightshirt, clutching a fork. You look around dazed. You don't even know where your power is.

Whether that realization hits ten seconds, ten hours, or ten days after you've been triggered, as you emerge from the fog of reaction, you may be tempted to criticize yourself. After all, haven't you cleared this stuff already?

Obviously not. And that's okay. Because this is all a process. But you can still leverage the experience. And, yes, you can reclaim your power. Days, weeks, or even months later.

THE POWER RETRIEVAL PROCESS

An exercise I call "the Power Retrieval Process" can take you there step by step.

Step #1: Anchor to awareness.

Take a quick moment to consider how you're approaching this Power Retrieval Process. Sometimes when we're in a place of pain or experiencing a trigger, we want to collapse into the cure and demand that we be fixed instantly. We want to feel better so we can get back to our usual ways of doing things. But accessing our true power isn't about returning to our usual ways of doing things. We're looking to see this unexpected trigger as a gift, to break through a pattern and take on a different role in our world. When you work through this process, you're not looking to feel better or get rid of anything, though that may be the end result. For now, you're simply shining the light of your attention on something that has, up until this moment, raged in the background.

Warrior, alchemist, leader. It doesn't matter which word you're using, but it's important that at the start of this process, you take a millisecond (yes, even if you're in heaps of emotions) to pause and make some gesture to anchor yourself to an intention of awareness, of seeing clearly. Not simply "fixing." (Plus, there's nothing to fix here. It's simply transmuting a power pattern that isn't even the truth anyway.)

Step #2: Make space.

Set your phone on "Do Not Disturb" and set the timer for at least ten minutes. You don't have to light candles, burn incense, invoke the spirits, or play music. Make this an uncomplicated, normal thing . . . because it is. Requiring some kind of spiritual "vibe" from ourselves or the setting to be "just right" is too much pressure and an excuse to give up. (FYI: I've done this process in dressing rooms and even at the gym between sets. Not kidding.)

Step #3: Do a body audit.

Check in with how your body feels from head to toe. Sense what's going on overall. How does it feel to be in this body that's yours? No need to label anything or rate anything. You're just doing kind of a "feel scan."

Step #4: Breathe.

As intentionally as possible, take four deep breaths. Inhale and exhale. Relax into them. Don't push or force. Don't worry if your mind keeps yammering, just breathe slowly and deeply.

Step #5: Inquire.

Now we're going to go back to the body. Remember the game we played with attention at the start of this section? It's kind of like that, but with the power moving around in your body.

And remember, there's no getting this right. There's no "nailing it."
So get back in touch with your body and ask it two questions.

Question #1: What?

As in: "What's going on here? What's this power, this energy that's so jarring and active right now?" Remember, you're not asking your mind this question. You're asking your whole body, your whole being. Sit with the question and sit with whatever your body tells you. It may feel awkward at first. Don't worry about it. This gets easier with time.

Question #2: Where?

As in: "Where is power going at this moment?" See if this shows you any part of your day that's incomplete, where you're getting obsessive, or where you want someone's approval. Try to visualize where the power is going. And try to limit how much your mind is tempted to say, "I'll tell you where it's going! It's going out to that bastard over at . . ." Your mind doesn't know. Patterns of power are much more subtle than what our minds tell us. Allow yourself to be led and just feel and observe.

You don't need to label the situation, the person, or the psychological issue that comes up. ("Oh, this is my childhood issue with my dad. I can see it." "This is me being an INFP! There it is again.") The challenge with power is that the mind wants to grab it and give it a label. But it's not a mind thing. It's a power thing. It's an energy thing. See if you can feel or sense (however it shows up for you) the quality of the power: Is it leaving? Going somewhere? Uncomfortable?

The weird thing here is that I can't tell you the right way to do this. Your power teaches you in the way you need to be taught. Your job is to sit and notice.

Step #6: Intend.

When you get even a small sense of the energy or power in the pattern—no matter what it's doing or what it feels like—see if you can invite your power back to you. Don't force, pull, or drag. We're dealing with something very, very subtle here. This is where you merely invite your power back to you and away from the situation, pain, person, or emotion that's draining it. Sometimes you can't tell exactly where it's going. Sometimes you can. No matter how you experience it, use your intention to invite it back.

You may feel something, you may not. Either way is fine. This is called practice, and we have to start somewhere. Don't make this a quick fix. It's better to do this imperfectly in short spurts until you begin to sense what your power is than to try to get it right.

Again, we are not "getting rid of" the stuff that we don't like. That's not the goal. The stuff we don't like is part of a pattern that has locked itself in place because of our constant resistance. Instead we're simply noticing, being curious, being with. Remember, power is not aggression or battle. It's much, much bigger than that.

THE PROCESS OF POWER

A guy walks down the street and falls into a hole. He spends the rest of the day pulling himself out.

Next day, he walks down the same street, falls into the same hole, spends the rest of the day pulling himself out.

Next morning, it's the same thing. Falls into that fucking hole again. Pulls himself out.

Next day, he walks down the same street, sees the hole, knows he needs to avoid the hole, barely gets around the hole, and falls in anyway. Takes him less time to get out now that he knows the ropes, but still, it's a pain in the ass.

Next day, he walks down the same street. He sees the hole. He works, sweats, and struggles. He manages to avoid the hole. Victory! He's exhausted the rest of the day.

Today he walks down another street.

When you're working with patterns of power, you're this guy. When you practice with awareness and intention, you shift old patterns. Patterns of struggle and of total untruth.

When a pattern releases, the part where you walk down another street isn't necessarily even a choice. It becomes instinct. You don't even go there at all. Your energy isn't drawn to it. Sometimes you don't realize the pattern has shifted until months later when you scratch your head and think, *Oh hey, that's gone. How about that?*

Also, now that you know more about your energy and your power, you don't need to label yourself as "easily triggered" or "overly sensitive." There is no need to use this as yet another way to identify yourself as broken, in need of fixing.

We're all working with our own power and energy. There's nothing special about it, or about the fact that you get triggered. In fact, the great thing about triggers is that they instantly show you when you're giving your power away. And soon, you'll both easily recognize and no longer be able to tolerate or ignore the feeling of being drained or muddled or fearful. You'll simply see these as pointers, as teachers—revealing yet another untruth and clearing obstacles from your way.

THE UNREMARKABLE REAPPEARANCE OF POWER

The Body Positive Headquarters, Berkeley, California, 5:45 PM

The weirdest thing was that it was dead silent.

Connie Sobczak always thought a moment this powerful should come equipped with some kind of mystical fireworks display. But there was none of that. No light shows. No nothing. Just a deep sense of peace that now filled the room.

When she'd first sat down on the cold floor of her office forty minutes earlier, Connie had felt consumed. By struggle. By drama. By the thing she called "my horrifying need for approval." But she sat still anyway, untangling the web of critical thoughts, examining all this emotion, curious about its hold on her. Slowly, she remembered who she was. That's when she watched everything transform as her very soul seemed to return.

As the sunset streamed through her office windows, bathing her in the warm glow, Connie was completely free for the first time in months. The clawing, clamoring pressure that had driven her every action had, without ceremony or applause, vanished. She smiled. Her choice was now simple and obvious.

That was Thursday.

On Friday morning, Connie made two calls. The first was to turn down what would have been more money than her nonprofit had ever received from a single grant. She officially withdrew the application she and her team had labored over.

The second call was to accept a different grant. A grant that had come easily and was a perfect fit. Still good money, but not as much.

The entire struggle had been about ego. A part of her had wanted the bragging rights of the bigger money. The name-in-lights recognition of a famous person validating her work. When word got out that this one Silicon Valley executive had expressed interest in her little nonprofit, the excitement had been stunning. Colleagues cheered her on, insisting this guy was her ticket, assuring her that getting his endorsement would be a turning point for her visibility and her work. The ensuing galas and dinners further fed the illusion.

Now Connie saw the high price that came when she and her team gave so much energy over to one man's approval—one executive who, until sunset yesterday, had been draining the life out of her.

To be fair, it was a game any nonprofit founder could get caught up in: "Here's my power, now write the check." And she had to admit, for a while there, she'd been an enthusiastic player. She cringed at the memory of one particular event when this guy had been vocally skeptical about an aspect of Connie's work, and she'd spent the evening trying to win him over, as if she were back in high school proving herself to the principal. The thought of it made her eyes sting with tears.

Here she was, a successful author and documentary producer. An advocate for body positivity and power. Cofounder of The Body Positive—a nonprofit that helped people connect with their innate wisdom and value themselves. An organization that had, in just a few years, become a resource to campuses, faculty, psychotherapists, and students all over the world, garnering awards and recognition at every turn.

So it was extra rich that in her zeal to further that cause, she'd stepped out of alignment with it. Handed over her power, and even turned on a little false charm. Funny how the cultural drive for success has a way of blinding us to our own patterns when they emerge, believing the personal work we've done—especially when we become leaders in the public eye—excludes us from the ranks of people who still get tripped up in their stuff. Connie marveled at how her inner work kept getting deeper, more subtle, and more important.

On Saturday, Connie was leading a training for a large group of psychotherapists and school counselors when the topic turned to vulnerability. Naturally, many were hesitant to confess their own struggles with body image and the pressures that came with the mental-health profession. A woman raised her hand and asked Connie about the very real challenge of seeing your own history played out in the patient's healing.

Connie's response was effortless and real: "This is a lifetime relationship—not just with patients and clients, but with ourselves," she said. "When we're called to serve others, we immediately become a part of the equation. An undeniable piece of the healing process. As we continue to heal ourselves, we ultimately heal others." As she said this, she got chills all over. Turns out, those mystical fireworks displays have their own timing.

INTERPRETING EXPERIENCES

13

SWORDS AND ARROWS: THE MEANING WE BRING TO EXPERIENCE

When I first moved to Asheville, I used to go to a cool little bookstore called Malaprops to write in my journal, drink ridiculous amounts of coffee, and eat this great little sandwich called the Italo Calvino.

One day, I struck up a conversation with the woman at the table next to me. She told me she read tarot cards. I'd never heard of tarot cards. She offered to do a reading on the spot. So I hopped over to her table and sat down in front of her.

She closed her eyes and prepared the cards. She handed them to me and told me to shuffle the deck. Then she took the cards back and held them for a moment in quiet concentration.

She set down the first card.

We both stared at it.

On the card was a man, face down in the dirt. There were ten swords in his back. Pools of his own blood formed puddles in the sand around his body.

We looked up at each other.

"This doesn't appear to bode well for me," I said.

I half expected her to stand up, collect the cards, brush off her pants, shake my hand, and say, "Well friend, it was nice knowing you. Good luck with this."

Instead, she smiled. "Well, that's one way to look at it, of course. But let me help you consider other ways to interpret this."

BUSINESS IS AN INTERPRETATION GAME

You always hear people say that business is a numbers game. Really, it's not. Business is an interpretation game. It's about gathering information, mining that information for meaning, and making decisions based on that meaning.

Let's say you hire someone who collects the data and tells you, "Last week, you had a thousand visitors to your website, and ten of them opted in to your mailing list." You are then left to interpret these metrics the only way they could possibly be interpreted: that 990 people found you unlikable.

What if, instead, you hire someone who collects the data and then interprets the meaning of the data? She shows you several places where links are broken or copy could be improved. She explains that these changes will dramatically optimize your conversion rates. Not once does she mention your unlikability. Amazing.

Everything is up for interpretation, of course. However, many of our reactions are fairly universal. Bleeding in the dirt with ten swords jammed into one's back? That would seem to indicate a pretty sizable failure. (And that at least *ten* people found you unlikable.)

My new friend the tarot reader smiled at my interpretation because it was predictable. That's how we've all been conditioned to see blades, blood, and betrayal . . . even if they are just pen-and-ink illustrations on four-by-six glossy stock paper.

Her take was different.

"I always find it interesting," she said, looking at my card, "that this guy has ten swords in his back. Why not just one? I mean, one gets the job done. After that, aren't we getting a bit dramatic?"

She paused to sip her tea.

"So that makes me curious about you," she said. "Are you prone to drama?"

I laughed.

She continued. "Because, yes, it looks like you've been through quite a bit of transition lately."

She was right on the money on both counts.

"And this card might be calling you to examine if you're exacerbating the situation with your translation of what happened. You may be focused on yourself as the hapless victim without also seeing the release and growth that's going on. That always makes things so much worse, don't you think?"

Ah. There she had me.

THE SECOND ARROW

In a teaching on suffering, the Buddha shared the difference between the pain that's caused by a wound of some sort and our reaction to that pain. The Buddha depicted the initial painful occurrence as the first arrow. The original hurt. The unexpected upheaval. We have no control over first arrows. First arrows happen all the time.

The second arrow is the one that causes your suffering. The second arrow is your judgment of the first arrow, or the knee-jerk reaction to your pain. Like, how you shouldn't be so sensitive. Or that you should be more evolved than this, what with all that therapy you've had. Or how this always happens to you. Or never happens for you. Or how those 999 website visitors finally discovered the truth: that behind it all, you are a total and utter fraud.

The Buddha's lesson is that the second arrow is optional—as is every arrow (or sword) thereafter. And that's the thing. That little tarot card could've propelled me into a paranoid spiral convinced of my impending doom. Or it could give me something to reflect upon and illuminate a truth for me. The interpretation—and thus the choice—was, and always is, mine. And it's yours, too.

OUT BEYOND BAD AND GOOD

Oprah Winfrey says your life is always speaking to you. So is your business. Maybe even more so. Your business is a constant feedback loop, showing you where you need to move, grow, let go, fire, rehire, or reposition. Your interpretation of that feedback determines your decision, which determines your next move. So whether it's your life or your business, if you don't know how to read and integrate that feedback—unfettered by second arrows—you end up creating messes. Or worse, getting stuck. Which is why it's imperative you become your very own wise tarot reader of sorts.

This requires the ability to see the context, access your intuition, and remember your intention, while pulling many angles into view. The mere fact of your humanness, however, means that you're fully equipped with a mind that wants nothing to do with stupid gray areas like context or intuition. Your mind wants order. Over the years, that mind has created a tidy little KonMari method of sorting your experiences into two neatly categorized bins: One labeled "good." (These are the things that make you happy.) The other labeled "bad." (These are the things that make you unhappy.)

Consider these four real-life experiences:

Experience #1: An employee steals $32,000. Bad. (Unhappy!)
Experience #2: A client signs on for a $100,000 contract. Good. (Happy!)
Experience #3: Several clients don't renew. Bad. (Unhappy!)
Experience #4: Your company surpasses its revenue goal. Good. (Happy!)

If you've never learned how to interpret experiences outside of their skin-deep appearance, then you'll place each experience into its appropriate good/bad bin, possibly missing its meaning and consequently its value to your business.

As a result, you'll spend a ton of energy avoiding the bad stuff. Judging the bad stuff. Perhaps collapsing when the bad stuff happens. And when good stuff happens, you'll cling to it like Gollum. In the time it takes to toast your success, you'll start worrying about screwing up and losing this great thing you just pulled off.

This is the way most of the world interprets experiences. In fact, if good and bad are your key measures of what happens in your business, you'll have plenty of company and commiseration.

As a Soul-Sourced Entrepreneur, however, your work is about vision and decision. It's about taking actions that uplevel your team, your company, and your clients. To support that intention, you need to be open and curious enough about your experiences—good or bad—to go deeper. To ask what's *really* going on here. To discover how this might inform your next move. To dig for interpretations that reveal how your experiences truly serve you, your business, and your intention, out beyond "bad" or "good."

With this in mind, let's take a closer look at the experiences mentioned above.

Experience #1: You fire the thieving employee. This leads to a heart-to-heart with your business partner. You discover you're blaming each other for this situation and a host of others. You meet for days and repair not just your employee interview process, but your relationship. Sure, you lost $32,000. But you prevented much bigger losses in the future.

Bad or good?

Experience #2: The $100,000 client turns out to be a high-maintenance nightmare. You realize that you were so ambitious to make such a big number that you ignored all the early signs of entitlement exhibited by this non-ideal client. You go way over budget on staff time (not to mention therapy).

Good or bad?

Experience #3: Losing those clients forces you to spend a quiet weekend analyzing who left and why. Doing so, you find the clients who didn't renew weren't aligned with the new direction you're taking your services starting next year.

Bad or good?

Experience #4: You hit your revenue goals only to discover you made zero profits. So you have bragging rights, but you made less money than you used to as a freelancer with a single virtual assistant.

Good or bad?

When you bring a deeper level of awareness to your experiences and interpret with an open, curious mind, you get a lot more than tidy containers filled with neatly aligned stacks of judgment. You get insight. You get direction. You get expansion.

YOU ARE THE CIO OF YOUR BUSINESS

What it all comes down to is this: You are the CIO of your business. The Chief Interpretation Officer. Your life, your business—in fact, all of your experiences—are meaningless in and of themselves. They happen. Each and every day, they happen. And they keep on happening.

But here's the kicker: Each one carries only the meaning you give it.

This may sound a bit intense. Like I'm setting you up for a nice little existential crisis here. I'm not. It's just that this is what trips up business owners all the time. It's that powerful.

In your business, if your intention calls for expansion (and they all do), then the experiences that follow are likely custom created by that intention to help you see, do, become, or let go of something your intention requires. So the opportunities and challenges in your business are your own personal set of tarot cards. As CIO, you're at the helm. You are the source. You are the alchemist. You assign the meaning. And you make decisions and take actions based on that meaning.

To grow and lead your business, then, you must become skillful at breaking out of autopilot, uncovering second arrows, and seeing experiences—good or bad—for the opportunity each one holds. From now on, you must be able to interpret each experience as something you initiated with your own intention in order to expand your world and your success. Only then, armed with this high level of awareness, can you truly move yourself and your business forward.

WHAT TO DO WHEN "HUSTLE HARDER" HURTS

It was a cold, cloudy New Year's Eve morning. Carolyn Connell held her coffee and stood at her office window watching the squirrel on the bird feeder. "Dude," she said aloud, "don't let my husband catch you."

Turning toward her desk, a paper on the wall caught her eye. Carolyn smiled, remembering how she'd tacked it up there the first week of January, almost a year ago. Somehow it didn't matter that it wasn't up to her usual exacting standards for design . . . the thumbtack had remained all year.

The paper was a written intention, complete with her signature. It had been her biggest intention ever. To have $200,000 in business revenue by, well, today, as a matter of fact.

She remembered the evening she signed it. She had been shaking. She'd always resisted talking about numbers and money, choosing instead to let her happy clients and her many Realtor of the Year awards be her main markers of success. But that night, she chose to stretch out of her comfort zone. Up until then, her largest annual income had been $130,000.

As she stood here today, she could look back and see how unaware she'd been of what exactly she was calling forth with the soundless scratch of her pen above the signature line.

The year had started swimmingly. She even got a little cocky. *Damn I'm good at this intention stuff,* she remembered thinking.

Then August happened.

Everything came to a halt. No matter what she tried, nothing worked. All of that cockiness drained out of her, replaced with a familiar committee of voices snickering, *Well, it serves you right, "Ms. All-That."*

By September, Carolyn was covered up in stories. She called them her greatest hits. They showed up whenever she'd set a big goal.

The first was a story about motivation and how it was a phony construct, designed to manipulate people into the illusion of hope. Inspiration was just a fleeting moment she had felt at a three-day retreat. When push came to shove, life didn't work like it did at three-day retreats. The second was a story about how her unique combination of flaws made it impossible for her to make a business grow like other people could. Her dad had been right all along. The third story was about the real estate industry. It was just a bunch of testosterone-driven men, who ignored the righteous and real people—the heroes—like Carolyn.

No amount of rational thinking had stopped the force field of these stories. They raged, attracting other related stories and random voices. A canceled lunch date with a friend turned into another internal flaw. A snarky email from a home buyer became a story of impending doom.

Until one day in mid-September, Carolyn couldn't get up off the sofa.

This is when her story became: What's the point?

She was at $112,000. Her goal was $200,000. Typically, her autumn months had been her slowest. She didn't have the energy to "hustle harder," which was the typical advice in this industry.

So now what?

With some help from her coach and mastermind, awareness kicked in. *Maybe*, she thought, *just maybe, I need to stop fighting, stop beating myself up, and start relating to my goal. I mean, this isn't a new pattern. In fact, this is why I avoid numbers. I'm really just avoiding myself.*

With compassion, she told herself, *I'm In.* The voices in her head wanted nothing to do with compassion. They wanted her to run faster and work harder. She did the opposite. Instead of desperately grasping after her goal, she simply pulled it closer to her. She renewed her relationship to it. (On one ceremonious evening, she even signed her intention again!)

She became aware whenever her behaviors were about checking out. Surfing the web. Blowing off meditation. Leaving her bed unmade. She was even tempted to cut hours for some of her team. But she didn't. Her only rule was not to run, give up, or play games about her intention.

Within a week or two, her power returned. She found herself naturally doing some of the grassroots marketing she loved. She took her assistant to lunch. She organized the office. When she caught herself obsessing about her goal, she would pause to breathe deeply. Then in October, she got a referral for a new client. Then another one. Effortless.

By November she was within $40,000 of her goal. Still unlikely that she'd reach it. But she was different now. She was already grateful to her goal for teaching her how to access her heart and a more unattached approach to intention. She was managing her energy in a way she'd never dreamed she could. She got four new clients in November—and then another one out of the blue in December, which had never happened before.

And on this day standing by her desk, coffee in hand, she proudly owned the fact that she had reached $208,000. The most she had ever made in her business.

On the day she first signed the intention, she thought the number would be the best part about it. But it wasn't. The best part was who she had become. She had trained herself to clear the stories that had, up until now, quietly ruled much of her life. She was grateful. And stronger.

And now, as a light snow started to fall and a lone squirrel blissfully ate the remaining seeds in the bird feeder, Carolyn pulled the tack and paper from the wall and sat down to set her intention for the coming year.

14

INTERPRETING FROM EXPANSION

O nce upon a time, I fell madly in love. This was just months after my post-college-boyfriend breakup. I was still at my cubicle job. Still writing letters to God in my journal about all my big music dreams.

And along came Doug.

It was one of those sweep-you-off-your-feet romances that goes from zero to 120 miles per hour in six seconds flat, leaving rational thought, or *any* thought for that matter, in its wake. During the thick of it, Doug—fresh out of college himself—left for South Africa for a year of volunteer work. He and I decided that in the summer when he had a break, I'd visit him for a month. We'd travel with the other volunteers in a rented van. We'd visit the coast. We'd camp. We'd have fun.

I decided to make a world tour out of making my way to South Africa. And in the weeks after our tearful goodbye on an icy January day, I got busy preparing for my adventure. I bought a big backpack and a stack of thick paper maps. I found someone to sublet my DC apartment. And, at long last, I quit my cubicle job at Ogilvy & Mather.

In the spring, I flew to Amsterdam and roamed, biked, and railed through the Netherlands, Belgium, and Germany. I made my way to Greece, where I camped on beaches and hung out in whitewashed villas perched above the Mediterranean. After that, I went on safari in Kenya and spent a few crazy days in Nairobi.

All the while, Doug and I sent airmail back and forth. I picked up his letters at preplanned destinations, waiting until I found the perfect café or sidewalk bench to open them and devour their contents, getting more and more excited for our reunion.

Finally, I flew to South Africa to be with my beloved . . . and he broke up with me in the rental car when we weren't even ten minutes outside of the Johannesburg airport.

INNOCENT BYSTANDER OR MASTER CREATOR?

Now, if you and I were in a café sipping Malbec, I could end this story right here. It might simply be a dramatic moment in my life that had no meaning beyond "hashtag men are assholes and romance sucks." You could even one-up me with your own story. We'd toast each other, agree we were done wrong, and admire the host of swords jutting out our backs.

But that's not where I go with this experience.

Sometimes I share my South Africa story with clients who are in major upheaval after they've initiated an intention for their business. That's because ultimately I didn't interpret this experience the way you might expect: me, the broken-hearted. Doug, the shithead. With space and stillness, I came to an interpretation of my experience that left me grateful (albeit somewhat bruised) for what happened.

Over time (lots of time), two major meanings emerged for me:

1. This was the answer to my prayer

Just months before I met Doug, I started writing all those letters to God in my journal asking for a bigger life, to leave the job I hated, to become a songwriter. Doug was simply carrying out the directives of my intention. (Turns out, our soul mates aren't always the ones who make us feel exquisite and comfortable.) Doug was extricating himself from a future where he didn't have a place. And he was sending me off to that future.

2. The trip to South Africa was the needed catalyst

Doug (and perhaps the hormonal response he generated) was the big push I needed to carry out my intention. It led me to quit my job with zero hesitation. Also, the trip itself and the solo travel were pivotal for me. A baptism of sorts. A waking up.

When I returned home, any dignified shred of my old self, any hope of keeping my ego intact, was pretty much destroyed. Friends and family saw me as broken, tilting their heads slightly, asking, "How you doin' there?" with furrowed brows. In anyone's eyes, I had little to lose.

So when the opportunity for a free apartment in another city came along, I went immediately. As people back home whispered about my mental stability, I found the time and the perfect community to nurture my music career.

I wouldn't have done any of it if not for Doug.

LESSONS VERSUS EXPANSION

In the end, I interpreted the experience as something I created. Something I initiated with my own intention that fiercely and forcefully expanded my life.

And that's not even the best part.

The best part is that no one can take my interpretation from me.

Doug could write his own chapter about this same experience. He could tell everyone *the truth*: that I was a needy puddle of a human who could barely spackle her life together, and besides that, a total drama queen with the self-awareness of a scallop.

My friends might've told me this experience meant I should get back to a normal life. Shake off my temporary insanity and recognize that my impulsive nature got me dumped. It was a good lesson. Time to put it behind me.

Valid as any of it might seem, it wouldn't matter. These would be *their* interpretations. *My* interpretation is all that matters here.

And my interpretation took a radically different approach. It was interpretation by expansion. This approach asks: How is this current experience expanding you? It asks you to look at the situation through the lens of what you've intended. To consider the possibility that the upheavals you're experiencing may have been created by that intention—even if they're unexpected or don't seem logical or connected at first.

This isn't how most people interpret. Most people do interpretation by judgment. The question they ask is: What's the lesson here? Which means that, from the get-go, your experiences are about slapping you down, showing you what you've done wrong. This model is based on the idea that we're tossed here on this planet to rack up lessons. As if life is nothing more than an angry church lady with one mission: to put you in your place and teach you a thing or two.

So you end up living your life with this low-grade panic, like a rat in some hideous experiment, terrified of getting shocked, trying your best to figure out the rules. And in a business, this only gets amplified.

If my question after my Doug experience had been, "What's my lesson?" I might have interpreted it like my friends did. As a disastrous result of my impulsive nature, proof that I walk a thin line on the spectrum of crazy. And that judgment-laden interpretation would have led to actions that were way out of alignment with my intention to become a songwriter. Namely, I would've given up and crawled back to my cubicle.

By asking, "How is this expanding me?" I found meaning that allowed me to use the experience for the catalyst it was.

When you stop expecting lessons and start mining for expansion, you automatically nix the judgment and get interpretations more likely to move you toward your intention. A subtle difference that makes all the difference.

15

HOOKED BY STORIES

As humans, we crave stories. Our brains are wired to tell them and hear them. Stories help us understand. They make facts interesting and memorable. They summon our emotions and drive us to action.

As business owners, we know that when it comes to marketing, stories rule the day. They keep customers riveted. And the best stories, the ones that grab us and suck us in, are the ones with clear-cut villains, victims, and heroes.

Consider what might arguably be called the best marketing moment of all time: Apple's 1984 Super Bowl TV commercial.

The scene opens with the voice of the villain: the evil dictator on that giant screen hypnotizing the masses with his propaganda. All around are his victims: the listless robotic look-alikes dutifully bound in their collective trance. In other words, the villain (IBM) was about to gain total control of a world of otherwise creative and vital human beings (you and me).

And then? Along comes our rescuer!

The girl hero. Complete with platinum highlights and aerobic gear. In her shiny, blonde colorful glory, she blazes down that hard, gray metal tunnel to save the day!

She is Apple. And when she flings her sledgehammer through the air and shatters the screen, breaking our trance, we all bond under one theme: *We were the victims! Now we're the heroes! Be one of us—go get yourself a Mac!*

Make no mistake. We love this shit. And there's nothing wrong with that! So teach with stories. Market with stories. Motivate and illuminate with stories. Lots of them. Douse your hair with Sun-In, grab a heavy mallet, and run fast as you can up that aisle of drones and take down that neo-fascist bastard!

But when it comes to interpretation, beware of stories. Those internal emotional dramas that have accumulated over a lifetime can permanently derail clear thought and any expansion-based interpretation.

In fact, if you've taken even a basic psychology class, you probably recognize the commercial's characters as points on Karpman's famous Drama Triangle, a social model of the roles we take on, especially when an interaction is stressful: The victim—the one who has been done wrong. The villain or perpetrator—the one guilty of the wrongdoing. Or the hero—the one who saves the day.

Adopting any of these roles in our real lives lands us smack in the middle of a story. And once we're energetically engaged in a story, we're hooked. We interpret our situation and every little movement from our character's point of view, not ours, and certainly not with an eye toward our expansion or intention.

As the story unfolds, we might shift into a different role in the triangle—perhaps we move from victim to hero (because we're never the villain, right?). But as long as we remain in that story, our actions are really nothing more than reactions—dictated by the story. No matter how right we are, how wronged we've been, or what we've done to save the day, there's no moving forward with clarity. There's only a perpetual wheel of drama. And more story.

Story isn't interpretation. It's pattern. It's emotion. Yet, some people build their entire business on this model, accumulating story after story, which then translates into reaction after reaction. This can be an especially easy trap to fall into for solo business owners, who don't have the gift of teams or partners to lend other perspectives.

THE STATUE OF LIBERTY BUSINESS

Pam's business was a heap of stories. Of course it was. As a consultant to nonprofits, Pam heard sad stories from her clients every single day. Stories of how little money they had, how hard fundraising was, of endless struggles, and of bad guys and good guys.

Pam felt sorry for her clients. They were victims fighting for victims. Pam was their rescuer. Doing all the heroic things a rescuer does. Discounting her prices, giving free consults over lunches, answering the phone at all hours, providing extra coaching days, working weekends and evenings. She was saving these poor people who were out there doing good in this cold, hard world.

Unconsciously, Pam had built what I call a "Statue of Liberty Business." An enterprise that pays homage to the famous sonnet at the Statue of Liberty's base: "Give me your tired, your poor, your huddled masses yearning to breathe free . . ."

An inspiring stanza for the United States of America's most revered port of entry, yes. But as a business model—not so much. Pam, like many business owners, was so attached to her need to rescue, to be the hero, that she forgot she was running a business.

Until the unthinkable happened (and not for the first time). One of Pam's bigger clients heard the siren song of another consultant's shiny new idea. And without even so much as a thanks, they emailed Pam and let her go. Worse, they didn't pay their invoice, which was huge. They'd continually put Pam off with a promise to pay her "someday." And Pam (being the hero to the tired and poor) had continued to work for them, counting on that promise.

Enter Pam's bitterness. And with it, role changes all around. The client who abandoned her became the villain. And now starring as the victim: Pam! She took to the new role like a pro. And with just the right levels of pissed off and indignant, she showed up on our coaching call. "I'm done," she announced. "I've decided to stop working with nonprofits. They're all struggling. They're clueless. I'm changing my whole business model, and I need you to help me."

When you're still reeling from an emotional hit, it's normal to interpret from the story. Pam's went something like this: "I work my ass off (me, the hero) for these people (them, the victims). And they ditch me (them, now the villains). This has happened more times than I can count (me, now the victim). I need to find people who appreciate my work (me, the hero).

I wanted to help Pam see beyond the story, to exit the Drama Triangle and find the clarity that would serve her growth. Otherwise, she'd be in danger of repeating the same pattern, no matter what model she thought she was building. So I asked her to play a game with me. I call it "ALT-5."

I said, "Let's see if you can come up with five alternate interpretations of what this situation might mean for you."

Pam was certain she knew exactly what had happened here, and most important, who was to blame. But she agreed to humor me.

I started by reminding her that she'd set an intention to double her revenue this year. Then I said, "What if your intention is actually manifesting here? What if it's pointing the way? This client has left you high and dry, and you have no signed contract for legal action. Where might your interpretation guide you? Give me five alternatives to 'nonprofits are clueless.'"

After several quiet moments, Pam sighed and said, "It could be that this particular group wasn't an ideal client. I mean, they couldn't even pay their invoice."

"Great," I said. "Keep going."

Another long pause.

"My intuition," she said, "had been screaming at me all along that I needed to stop working until they paid me. Plus, I saw weird emotional dynamics happening all around. So I guess this could be showing me to stop, to trust my intuition, and to communicate when I start feeling 'off' in a client relationship."

"Perfect. What else?"

"Well," she started after another long pause, "if I look at why I kept working and working, I think it's because I don't value myself very much. So there's that."

"So, you might need to be present enough to notice where you devalue your services and time?"

"Yes," she said.

"Got it," I said. "Gimme two more."

"Well, now that I'm looking at it, I guess I don't really treat my business very professionally. I'm scattered. And I don't take the time to set things up, like, I didn't even have a contract for this client. Who does that?"

Now we were getting somewhere.

"And it could be that I need to evaluate my client onboarding process, and create some standards and expectations for who I work with and what I do."

Even though her voice had gotten small, Pam obviously felt the clarity of these alternate interpretations. She said, "Okay, this feels lighter. Like I can take steps and make some positive changes." Then she added, "But it also feels scary."

Scary is often how it feels when you find a true interpretation, one that expands you. That's because you've finally come face-to-face with your story and the dark (but familiar) pattern that's been keeping you stuck. You can no longer deny that it's within your power to change this dynamic for the better because now you know the way. And that means there's deep, and yes, uncomfortable work to be done. It seems easier to just ditch the whole thing and start over. But that's just part of the same old pattern.

THE ALT-5 PRACTICE

When you find yourself in a tough circumstance in your business—and perhaps caught in a story—you can lead yourself through ALT-5.

Before you begin, take a moment to recall your intention. Then consider the situation you're currently facing and respond to the prompts below. Remember, there are no right or wrong answers—just curiosity and expansion.

1. I wonder if it's possible that . . .

"I wonder if it's possible" is a simple opening that eases us out of judgment and begins to engage curiosity. This simple switch can be illuminating. Wonder is the key here.

2. Maybe I'm being called to . . .

How might this circumstance be calling you to wake up or improve a skill in order to manifest the intention you initiated?

3. This could be expanding me by . . .

Let's ditch the worn-out idea of "lessons." Consider instead that you're breaking out of old paradigms and patterns by taking new actions that are outside your comfort zone.

4. An objective observer might see this situation and simply point out . . .

As much as you might despise clichés, they often contain some undeniable truths. Like when your entrepreneurial friend says, "Hey, that's just the cost of doing business," and you want to punch him. Sometimes it really is that simple. What's a basic observation that an outsider might have of this situation?

5. If the emotional "charge" of this trigger were magically reduced by 78 percent, here are five possible action steps I could take . . .

Imagine a team of "energy doctors" could enter this picture. Imagine that while you sleep or futz with your phone, they could surgically remove the emotional charge from the situation. Like, they extract all the drama. Your emotions are reduced by 78 percent. What are five steps you could take if this were the case? This is just a simple way to train your brain to leave the energy of the story behind as you consider solutions and doable actions.

To download a supremely cool printable copy of ALT-5 and other tools in this book, visit www.SoulSourcedBook.com.

The gift of practicing ALT-5 is that it trains you to walk through the door marked "exit" on the Drama Triangle. It cultivates a new awareness, teaching you it's possible to operate at a higher level, no longer allowing a situation or another person to define who you are, what you think, and what you do. You take responsibility for yourself, your responses, and what a circumstance means. It's the direct experience of no story. Until you've embodied this freedom for yourself, it might seem elusive or even impossible to imagine.

CLEAR LEADER OR COLD-HEARTED SNAKE?

In fact, whenever I refer to the victim-villain-rescuer drama that drives bad business decisions, inevitably someone in the room gets pissed.

They go to the mic. They get puffed up. They say, "So, you just want us to be cold? To ignore real victims? What about all the awful stuff in history? What about Hitler? Or Mussolini? Real villains are out there!"

If this is what's happening in your head right now, let's pause.

I'm asking you—on a personal level—to consider how drama might be ruling your business. Notice the sneaky ways your mind ensures that you never have to experience the discomfort of relinquishing this pattern. Your mind builds a sweeping unwinnable argument (a.k.a. story) for why drama must continue to rule you. Because otherwise—it so brilliantly argues—you'll be a fascist. (Along with everyone who isn't ruled by the Drama Triangle.)

So, first off, it's awesome that you don't want to harm other people. I love that about you. But take a moment to see if you've conflated social and political justice issues with your personal drama and gotten all mixed up and mashed up inside as a result, using big, painful ideas to keep yourself trapped at a low level.

The hard truth is this: Taking responsibility is the ultimate freedom. Taking responsibility is not taking blame. It is saying that these are your circumstances as they are. It's owning the truth of your situation. And then asking yourself what comes next. No, you won't suddenly discover the answers to all of the world's suffering and pain. But you will become a healthy leader operating from a place of clarity. A place where you can act purposefully. A place where you take personal responsibility (not blame, mind you) for your results, actions, and experiences. For some people, like Pam, this is nothing less than a miracle.

16

ACCESSING NEUTRAL

Ideally and ultimately, we want to interpret our business experiences from a place that's unencumbered by stories and emotional baggage. A zone of curiosity and possibility, where clarity has space to emerge. I call that zone "neutral."

Depending on how you're wired, the idea of neutral may feel totally impossible. It's so distant from how we've been conditioned. It may even be a bit underwhelming in its simplicity. There's no reaction, no drama, no righteous indignation to grab us by the shoulders and show us the way. In essence, neutral is a return to nothing. And as such, it's an opportunity to see everything as it is.

"Neutral" is tricky for anyone who's sensitive or feels deeply. On one hand, it's so appealing. It sounds like some magic cape you put on and finally get "rational," like everyone's always told you to be. Like you'll suddenly see things through the logical eyes of your engineer brother, who randomly texts you quotes from *The Daily Stoic*. However, it can also feel like yet another rule demanding that you stop being so damn sensitive. Or stop feeling at all.

This is *not* what neutral is about. In fact, let's back up real quick.

THE PART WHERE I TALK ABOUT FEELINGS

When my South Africa breakup happened, I didn't shift gears instantly, get to neutral, and interpret the experience as the answer to my intention. Quite the opposite. I was a hot mess. I paced and sobbed and paced and sobbed into the wee hours, night after night, listening to a playlist of songs too embarrassing to recall. (Think Journey.) I was uninvited from the group of volunteers Doug and I were supposed to travel with. I had to figure out four weeks in a foreign country on my own. Add to that the very public embarrassment of making such a long trip only to get rejected.

Even after I returned to the States, my heart was raw. I was floored by blasts of shame and self-doubt that could bring me to my knees at any random moment. But I let myself experience these feelings. That's how I was able to then move onward and into the clear interpretation, which *is* what neutral is about.

Emotional pain sucks. But for many of us, it's just part of the ride. And in your business, where your ideas, creativity, and financial wellness are at stake, the ego deaths you experience are real. So before you can refocus on your intention, reclaim your energy, or have a hope in hell of skillfully interpreting anything, you may need to make space for your emotional responses.

Here's why: When a strong emotion hits you, you're likely dealing with something deep, something unconscious. And often, it's something that won't provide you with a valuable interpretation—though it will certainly try. So when a strong emotion is there, it's your signal to pause. Stop doing. Stop working. Stop figuring. Stop trying to be stoic. Stop trying to fix anything. And definitely stop interpreting.

Emotion is often unresolved energy from old stuff in your past. I tell my clients that life is high school and then getting over it. This makes them laugh, but it's a laugh of recognition. When you were navigating your childhood or teen years, most likely you didn't have the tools—and often you didn't have a support system—to help you manage the things that hurt. And if those unresolved things are now the backdrop for interpreting your experiences, you end up with a seventeen-year-old running your business. This usually doesn't work out so well.

Add to that the well-worn attitude that says you aren't supposed to *have* any feelings as a business professional (or, let's be honest, if you hope to be counted among the spiritually elite). Talk about emotions or feelings and you officially become a "girl" (or, more politely, "have feminine values") in the business world, where anything even resembling a feeling is stuffed, shamed, or hidden away. And any mention of heart or tears nets you an uncomfortable clearing of throats.

In business, if feelings are talked about at all, they often get that convenient Law of Attraction spin, where you're jettisoned into a positive frame of mind with lightning speed. As in, *let's not get ourselves uncomfortable here with any of those messy feelings you seem to be having.*

Yet, the problem remains. In our attempts to avoid, gloss over, or stuff emotion, that energy has nowhere to go. And as we have already learned: energy doesn't lie. So it ends up accumulating and operating beneath the surface—mucking up our clarity and speaking louder than our game of pretending.

THE PART WHERE YOU OWN A BUSINESS AND FEEL AT THE SAME TIME

None of this is conscious, of course. It happens below the surface in the blink of an eye.

Even when we believe we're letting an emotion be felt, we're often not. We're thinking, explaining, rationalizing, trying to put the feeling in a category and make it make sense. To fix it. We use this as another way to distance ourselves from discomfort.

When we *think about* our emotions, rather than simply experience them, we lock that energy in place. Any thoughts, judgment, and finger-pointing we attach to our feelings ultimately weigh down the original feeling, keeping it stuck and unable to move on.

This is what Jill was doing in the face of rejection.

Jill poured her heart and soul into a pitch to a prestigious corporation that had placed her on a "short list" of potential vendors. She spent months preparing. She did a stellar job at the presentation. She thought she had it locked. But the six men around the conference table chose someone else. That someone else happened to be a man.

Jill was devastated. She called me just hours after she got the news. As she talked, I noticed she wasn't truly feeling the sadness. Instead she was talking about and around her sadness.

There was outrage: "Those bastards only wanted a man. They're total sexists. They wasted my time. I'm too good for this shit."

There was shame: "I'm too strong to act like this. What's wrong with me? I'm so embarrassed."

And self-criticism: "I could've done a better job. What did I miss?"

Yes, these are all feelings. The problem was that she wasn't letting herself experience the real pain. The root pain. The very normal heartbreak of working her ass off and not getting the bid.

I waited until Jill had worn herself out. When there was a pause, I assured her that I'd eventually help her interpret this experience clearly. But not yet. I offered that, for now, she let herself feel the grief. I shared that when we don't let ourselves just hurt, when we stuff the plain-old raw emotion, we accumulate an internal resistance that can become a hard veneer around our creative ventures.

"So you mean, you want me to just be sad about being rejected?" Jill said. "Just to be sad for that?"

"No, Jill. This isn't about me wanting you to be sad or asking you to manufacture sadness. You *are* sad. I just want you to *experience* the sadness that's already here. It's completely normal to feel grief about losing something you really wanted."

Then I told Jill about a secret weapon of mine. It's a practice I call "Going Fetal."

FETAL BEFORE NEUTRAL

Going Fetal is simply giving yourself permission—in this fast-paced, often aggressive world of business—to truly feel what you need to feel without all the stories and thoughts and judgments attached to it. By yourself. Without enrolling others in the stories and thoughts and judgments. (Rehashing your emotional event with a friend over and over again may trap you both in a story, keeping your pain alive rather than releasing it.)

I started this practice back in my songwriting days, when rejection was not an uncommon experience. Sometimes it would roll off of me, which made me proud, like I was finally a badass. Other times, not so much. The rejection would break my heart. Whenever I tried to pretend it didn't or attempted to "grow a pair" (as one music executive advised), I'd end up feeling contorted, with a low-grade resentment. I'd become resistant to the work, to myself, and my creativity.

So I'd "Go Fetal." (To me, the name brought some lightness to the practice and kept it from being some heavy-duty spiritual mandate.) When I went fetal, I gave myself the space to feel completely and utterly broken. And, if necessary, to curl into a ball under the covers.

There are three steps to Going Fetal.

1. Spot the emotion.

This is the tricky part. To spot the emotion means you must pause long enough to recognize when something hurts. In the name of being an adult or having a busy schedule, most of us keep driving forward without realizing that we're in pain. So we're operating out of reaction to that pain. Plus, our judgment of pain can ensure we never, ever admit to having it or mastering the ability to be aware of our own body and what it's experiencing.

Spotting the emotion can happen the instant you feel the hit. Or you can catch yourself in behaviors that reveal something's out of balance—you shout at your daughter, or you elbow someone out of the way at Trader Joe's. Shame might arise as a result of these actions, and it might be the first sign that something's off. If you give yourself a moment here, you might recognize these behaviors as symptoms and begin to explore what's underneath.

That's hard to do if you're accustomed to driving forward regardless of how you feel. Becoming aware of your heart is a subtle art. It can be an enormous burden. Like being late for a wedding when you're the maid of honor, and you have to stop at the store with your toddler who stages a total meltdown in aisle three and refuses to move, oblivious to the fact that people are waiting on you and that you have the wedding rings.

Toddlers don't do rushes. Neither do emotions. Until we bring intention and presence to an emotion, it'll continue to operate in the background. The good thing about being an adult is that if you spot the emotion at an inconvenient time—like during a meeting—you can acknowledge it, you can say, *I see you,* and you can let it know you'll be available later to be present to it.

2. Create the container.

This is where you define the parameters. When you can be present to the emotion, I recommend setting a timer. And yes, when I do this practice, I literally set a timer. Sometimes it's for twenty minutes. If something really hits hard, I might set it for an hour. The time itself doesn't matter. We're simply creating space. Not a rush. A container to be present with something important.

3. Experience the emotion.

This is when I tell myself, "Okay, have at it. Feel the hell out of this thing." I either sit on the floor or crawl into bed. No matter where I am, I just let whatever needs to be felt be felt. When thoughts arise *about* the emotion, I let them move on. I have a genuine curiosity about the sensation that *is* the feeling. I know that the feeling alone is what I'm seeking and allowing, not all the stories about my inevitable demise or perpetual brokenness. I find the feeling itself and just let it do what it needs to do. When the alarm sounds, I tell myself I did a great job. I say, "Time's up!" Then I get up and kindly gauge what activities—if any—I need to do next.

It may sound stupidly easy. But this is the very thing we're all clamoring to avoid. When you simply *feel* that feeling, when you explore that terrain, it becomes exactly what it is: a sensation. And it loosens up because it finally has a safe space to do that.

Obviously, there's no guarantee that when the timer dings, your feelings will have moved on. As much as your typical executive would like that to be the case, you can't time your breakdowns. But with the practice of Going Fetal, you get to make the space and time to feel the feeling, instead of stuffing it or judging it.

Bonus Step

I almost didn't include this step. I was concerned that some people might be tempted to jump right to it—forgoing the work of the prior three steps. Just so you know, this step is of no value unless and until you have worked your way completely through Going Fetal.

So with that caveat, this bonus step is one of simple curiosity. The aim is to give the emotions you've just felt even more space to lose their charge.

After you've finished Going Fetal, take a moment. Sit quietly. Ask yourself: What might really be going on here? What's all this emotional energy about? Ask these questions with curiosity. Without judgment. And without the need for a direct answer. You're not trying to make the emotion, the situation, or anything all better. You're simply observing it and letting it be.

For me, this bonus step further loosens any leftover attachment to the feeling. The very act of asking the questions diffuses emotion. Eventually, it becomes little more than a sensation to me. I begin to enter neutral, where I gain perspective and clarity.

THE PART WHERE YOU TRUST YOURSELF

Going Fetal is about having permission to just experience the *energy* that is the emotion. Not the story we've told ourselves forever about this emotion. It gives emotions the attention they need, holding them in our awareness. Freeing them from the clutches of our thoughts.

When we experience them, a few things happen. For one thing, you start to trust yourself. You begin to trust that there's a container for this stuff, there's a safe space within you for these scary feelings to move. Also, the sensation itself often "thins out." It loses its power to overtake you. In my experience, it returns less and less, and it takes up less and less time with its demands. This is how we create the often-touted and ever-elusive trait of resilience. This is how we become confident and start to trust ourselves.

Through consistently facing and feeling your feelings, you create a heart and mind that are ready for anything. It doesn't mean you won't feel emotional pain. It just means that when you do feel it, you're going to feel it in a way that doesn't harm you or harm others . . . or worse, keep that pattern locked into place forever.

As a corporate trainer with a strategic mind, Jill was skeptical of this odd little "Going Fetal" practice. But she humored me and tried it. An hour here. Fifteen minutes there. And even once during a quiet pause at a stoplight when the hurt showed up again. When we talked a week later, she reported feeling genuinely lighter. "I always thought success meant having a tough outer shell," she said. "I'm finally seeing that it has more to do with being in flow and moving forward with an open heart. It makes me un-scared of myself."

FIXING, GETTING RID OF, AND MAKING IT ALL DISAPPEAR

Hold on. You want me to just sit with pain and not try to fix it? Not try to get rid of it? Well that's just stupid.

If this is what you're thinking, I get it. You have a point. What I'm asking you to do here is the exact opposite of, well, everything. Every single technique and tactic—from EFT to NLP to nootropics to affirmations—is about *getting the fuck out of pain*. We want to fix things. We don't want to hurt. And we don't want to revel in our hurt—because then we'll just be whiny and morose. Or like your crazy Aunt Leona.

First off, when you're present with emotion, you're not reveling in it. We revel in it only when we connect a story to it and then replay it on an automatic mind loop. And when we're present with emotion, we do not become whiny and morose at all. We lighten up.

Years ago, I regularly babysat a little boy named Nathan. Once, when he was learning to walk, he took a few steps with his fuzzy socks on—and he slipped before I could grab him. He fell onto his chin. First, there was that initial look of surprise. And then that unmistakable frozen-face-baby-inhale that precedes an all-out explosion. Which is exactly what happened. Nathan screamed at the top of his little lungs. It was awful. There was blood all over his chin. I panicked. I yelled for his dad, who had just headed out the door, and he rushed right back in.

What I witnessed next still stays with me to this day.

Nathan's dad sat down on the floor right next to Nathan as he screamed. He pulled his son to him and said, just very matter-of-factly, "Hey buddy, that was pretty scary wasn't it? I totally get it. You're doing big things now with all this walking. And sometimes, when you're trying big things, stuff happens. And you know what? That's kinda normal."

He didn't try to change Nathan. He didn't tell him to "shhhhhh" or feel better. He didn't do EFT or NLP or coat the whole thing with a pretty story. He was simply *with* his son in his pain, seeing it, acknowledging it.

In less than a minute, Nathan was quiet. He was breathing and looking curiously at the blood on his fingers. Then he looked up at his dad, and he broke out into this big huge smile. As if to say, "You're right! I *am* doing big things here!" And just like that, the incident was done, and the bandage was on his chin.

Hey, I like energy techniques. They have a place. People do cool things with NLP and EFT practices. The problem is that the motivation behind the technique is often: "Get out." "Fix it." "Get rid of this shit." Or a denial of our natural responses and states. When that's the driver, the intention of "get this out of here" becomes yet another resistance to what is. And in the long run, resistance doesn't shift anything.

I think of the occasional toddler I see in a grocery store who falls or does something silly and ends up crying. The parent grabs the child, yells at him, tells him he should've known better—or worse, shakes the child and says "stop it." And the child—if he can control it—stops breathing. Holds it down. Nothing moves or releases or heals.

This is not a dialogue about parenting or inner children. But it does point to how we handle something as simple as emotional energy. Especially when it doesn't feel simple. It feels like we need to contort, control, beat it down, stuff it, ice over it with a million affirmations, pretend it's not there. Or shame it for being there at all. But none of this helps it move—especially when you're working with an old emotional pattern.

So the next time you sit with an emotion, don't sit with it with the intention of getting rid of it. If you can, sit with it with presence and curiosity and compassion. Exactly as Nathan's dad did.

Look, this is your business. It's your creation. No matter how badass, kick ass, or wiseass you are, your heart will get broken. You can never know what will or won't succeed. Like Jill, you may work your butt off for months on something only to lose, get rejected, or experience failure. Yes, clear interpretation will follow. And with it, the necessary resilience. But first, let the pain be there.

The experience of accessing neutral and how long it takes to get there will vary with every emotion and situation. That's okay. Because you can't demand your way into neutral, any more than you can fight and clamor your way to inner peace. You have to let things move and evolve in their own time. To allow anything that's not neutral to lose its fearful grip on you.

In other words, you must feel what you feel so it can stop unconsciously driving you. When that emotion finally lets go and you find yourself in a neutral space, the highest interpretation—and the right solution— will be there, too.

"I GOT THIS": FROM PANIC TO POWER IN FOURTEEN MINUTES FLAT

Triana Cordoza had heard the expression "dropping a bombshell" many times. Her clients often used it to describe the unexpected news or shattering announcement that landed them at her law practice, seeking her counsel.

Now she was experiencing it firsthand. From her own husband.

Her initial thoughts went something like this: "Panic! Panic! Panic!" (Like the *Lost in Space* robot. *Danger! Will Robinson!*)

Other thoughts tried to drown out the fear and take the high road: *Be a good wife! Support your husband! He's wanted this for years!*

Then there was the lone bitchy thought. *Hello? A heads-up here might've been nice. Like, let me in on your plan so I could, you know, prepare?*

But there was no reason to express any of this out loud. At least not here in the foyer as she arrived home, still holding her bags and briefcase as her husband shared his big news.

After all, this was inevitable. All those late nights at the kitchen table, listening to his frustrations. "I'm so unhappy. This company has no ethics to speak of. I can't keep working like this."

Someday, they'd agreed, he'd have to quit.

And Triana was discovering someday was today. *Bombshell.*

With no warning, Triana was now the official family bread-winner. She *so* wished she could cheer for her husband. She wanted to be able to say all the right things like, "I got this." Or, "You take the time you need to find the perfect job." Or, "I love you and you deserve this."

But standing in the foyer, Triana simply froze. She plastered a surprised smile on her face as her husband replayed the events of the day in a blur. Something about a partner making excuses again and creating more tension on the team . . .

Only two years ago, Triana had been in his shoes, leaving the grueling hours, rigid industry culture, and secure paycheck of a prestigious law firm to start her own practice, Cordoza Legal Group. With her husband supporting her, she worked hard developing the skill sets and resilience required for busi-ness ownership.

When you go to law school, they teach you how to be a

lawyer, not how to be an entrepreneur. And Triana, an avid researcher and fierce advocate for her clients, was a kick-ass attorney. She knew that much. But business had been a whole new muscle.

Shedding industry norms, she designed a practice aligned with her values and style. She'd even traded in the standard navy-blue suit, for (shocker!) colorful scarves and dresses. To her delight, it was working. In the last year her practice got legs and started to operate at a profit. Her confidence was on the rise. She'd even started getting calls from other small firms to ask her what she was doing and how she was making it all work.

But this? This was a whole new level. Could her practice really support the household while her husband took the needed time to find a new position?

The thoughts in her head—the very ones that made her a whip-smart attorney, scoping out every possible angle, problem, and obstacle—were clear in their final verdict: *No. Freaking. Way.*

That's when she did something radical. She set down her bags and held up her finger as her husband was about to share more details that led to his big, bold move. "Hold on," she said, and kissed him. "I need about fifteen minutes in my office. Is that okay? I'll be right back out."

Once in her office, she sat at her desk chair. She was shaking. Her heart was pounding. Her mind was reeling.

She told herself to breathe. She let the raging thoughts run their course, remembering that her brilliant mind didn't always have the answers for every situation. She did the very thing she always did for her clients: She got to neutral.

Then, when the pressure had eased up, she logged on to her computer and studied the numbers. Releasing images of bombshells and doom, she relaxed. *Okay,* she thought. *I can do this. I can be the breadwinner. And we can still go on our vacation. The rest is all mindset and owning my truth.*

After sitting quietly for another few minutes, she went to

the kitchen where her husband was waiting at the table. He looked up at her nervously. She said, "Know what? I got this. You take the time you need to find the perfect job. I love you and you deserve this." Then she sat down and smiled. "Now, tell me everything."

17

THE HABIT OF INTERPRETATION

Andy Forch, cofounder of the iconic Huckberry catalog, says, "Entrepreneurs aren't born. They're made." True that. Whether artist, healer, designer, attorney, or adventure-seeker, no one is a "natural entrepreneur," blessed with the ability to interpret from intention or toward expansion. This is challenging stuff we're doing here. So you're not alone if you wonder if you should give it all up or if you're missing some kind of "business" gene. You shouldn't, and you're not. This is a muscle. And the great thing about muscles is that they can be trained.

But it's all in the practice. The training.

A long time ago, I discovered a way to build the interpretation muscle. This was when my music career was growing. I realized that no one was going to discover me or rescue me. *Damn.* I faced the stark reality that I'd have to be the steward for my work in the world. And I'd have to build an actual successful business around my creativity. Which meant I'd have to become a stronger owner of that business.

I created a practice—and a tool—to give me some space. Let me see my business as a whole. And put me in a neutral mindset to make decisions about the upcoming week. It was my own little "come to Jesus" meeting, where I got quiet and brought some perspective to my fast-growing business. Best of all, it was simple.

I set twenty minutes aside on Sunday mornings. Then, I'd begin the ritual by acknowledging my accomplishments. This was crucial. It's all too easy to keep driving forward without celebrating little victories and expansions. To that end, I made myself write down even the smallest achievements.

After that, I'd release the clutter in my mind. I'd review stuck spots. I'd list my current challenges. Then, seeing all of it there in black-and-white, I'd set intentions and priorities for the coming week.

It wasn't a task list or a day planner. There were no colors and tabs to keep myself in perfect mental order. It was simply a gentle nudge back to my intention. A moment of perspective I came to count on week after week.

After a month or so of this habit—which I would end up naming "the Sunday Summit"—I noticed something radically different about myself. I was clearer. I was calmer. And I looked forward to Sundays and having this time to review the week and think about my business.

In time, the Sunday Summit was the real deal. And as I moved into coaching, I formalized it and taught it to Uplevel clients.

It quickly became an addiction for many of them. A really good addiction.

It's a simple habit that brings you back to center each and every week. It's also a record with data points—allowing you to deepen your perceptions, nurture your intuition, and build that interpretation muscle.

Over the years, the Sunday Summit has grown and improved, thanks to all the Uplevel clients who embraced it and provided feedback and results. Here's the tool in its current form and how to use it.

THE SUNDAY SUMMIT

Set aside about twenty minutes on a Sunday to quietly focus on your business. To me, Sundays work best because you're not yet caught up in the workweek minutia, and you have sacred space for clarity. In your journal, or a dedicated notebook, write your responses to the following questions.

1. What I accomplished, attracted, or "aha'd" this week . . .

Acknowledge even the slightest victories you achieved in the past week—a finished project, completed invoices, overcoming fear, or following up on a sales call. Doing this weekly creates an awareness of how much you accomplish and how many obstacles you break through. Things that go right often don't get the focus they deserve. And they need to. When you bring awareness to your achievements, it strengthens your knowledge base, and it feels good. It helps you align with your abilities, even (and especially) if the week seems to have gone off the rails.

2. Something I wanted to accomplish but didn't . . .

If you're like me (and everyone else on the planet), there are items you keep intending to do, and for some reason, you don't get to them. When you bring awareness to those items, themes will emerge. You'll notice what you're avoiding, putting off, or forgetting.

Instead of wasting your energy on judgment, you'll notice patterns. You'll interpret. You'll discover what's really going on and why. For instance, maybe this item keeps showing up week after week, and you realize it's not the right time to accomplish it. With that deeper insight and self-awareness, you can rearrange your priorities or set it aside entirely until later in the year and stop berating yourself.

3. Three things that could have made this week even better . . .

This is where you'll coach yourself toward alternative responses or work habits or any other changes you might make. This is not about judgment or wishful thinking. Instead, this is where you see when you might have gone unconscious and, here in this more intentional moment, you can shift into more supportive behaviors. This wires you toward clearer responses next time around.

4a. One challenge I'm facing . . .

You're facing many challenges. I know that. But listing every single gripe and challenge is a surefire way to create panic and hysteria. You can't solve them all. And you certainly can't solve them all in a week. So pick a single challenge. Then articulate it in a way that's clear and not covered up in drama. The ability to articulate challenges clearly is a skill set and a victory in and of itself. Knowing how to clarify what the challenge is trains your brain out of helplessness and overwhelm, and into actionable steps.

4b. How might this challenge be calling me to expand?

Now your practice of weekly interpretation really takes off. Articulating and interpreting smaller challenges weekly helps you become masterful at interpreting the bigger challenges when they arise. When the stuff that happens each week no longer brings you down but propels you forward, you begin to trust yourself as an interpreter. And so, when the proverbial shit hits the proverbial fan, you have faith in your ability to interpret for the highest meaning and outcome.

5. Are there any unmade decisions on my plate?

Nothing drains your energy and your brainpower more than unmade decisions. Putting things off can eat away at your ability to think clearly because in the back of your mind, you're still ruminating and not taking action. We'll dive into decision-making in the next section of this book. But for now, tuning in to any decisions you've put off will wake you up to where you might needlessly be spinning your wheels. Again, it's all training the awareness of your patterns.

6. Top three priorities for the coming week . . .

Based on the momentum you've created and the challenges you're facing (or in spite of those challenges), name your top three projects or actions for the coming week. This is not a to-do list. These are key areas on which you want to focus your energy the very most.

7. The one "make-me-proudest" priority above all else . . .

Choose one of your three priorities and make it king. This is the one thing you'll get done no matter what crisis hits this week. No matter if your kid gets hurt on the playground at school and you need to pick him up and care for him the rest of the day. No matter if your assistant gets sick, leaving you to deal with menial tasks for two days. Whatever happens, you will shift your priorities and get this one thing done that will make you proud.

8. My one-word theme for the week . . .

Choosing a word of the week helps to anchor you to your intention for the next seven days. Sometimes it will be a reminder word (focus, clarity, strength), sometimes an energizing word (faith, resilience, delight), and sometimes it's the same word you chose last week. Choose a word that anchors you.

The Sunday Summit is part of all Uplevel You programs and masterminds. And hands down, it's the most used and loved of all our tools. That's because it touches all four stages of the Soul Track. If you use it religiously, over time, you'll become clearer and clearer about your business and yourself—freeing your energy, improving the quality of your intentions, interpretations, and decision-making, and creating a mindset for success.

To download a supremely cool printable copy of The Sunday Summit and other tools in this book, visit www.SoulSourcedBook.com.

STOCK PHOTOS AND SMALL FLOCKS OF SHEEP

It was a crazy cold overcast day in March. I was tucked away in my office writing website copy, trying to ignore that winter wasn't budging.

My operations director knocked. It was tax time, and I had to sign some checks. One for the IRS. And one for the North Carolina Department of Revenue.

It had been a fantastic year for Uplevel You. We'd stretched, launched, grown, hired, reached goals, broken records, and moved into multiple seven figures in revenue. We'd even stashed money away in a special account just for taxes.

In fact, if the world worked the way advertisers want you to think it does, I'd be one of those executive ladies in the stock photos. The one sitting at her laptop in a clean white room all alone pumping her fists in the air, throwing her head back, and laughing uproariously at how much ass she just kicked.

At the very least, you'd think this wouldn't be anything challenging. Sign the checks and be done with it, right?

But when those checks were set down in front of me, my stomach jolted. The amount I was sending off to the government totaled $269,000.

In my mind, I could hear my mother gasp, *Good God, Christine, you could buy a house with this!*

I could see the touring musician I was—not all that long ago—hauling my gear into a ground-level room at the Super 8, unable to imagine making, let alone *spending*, a number even a fraction of that size.

I recalled a friend getting a number-one song on *Billboard* and telling me his first royalty check was "a quarter-million bucks!" Which, at the time, sounded like "set for life" money.

It hit me that I was about to casually sign two checks equaling an amount that was astronomical to that former self, who I now pictured walking gingerly across that motel room on the sides of her feet in a feeble attempt to avoid whatever unspeakable horrors had spilled, splattered, and coagulated onto the carpet.

In an instant, tears filled my eyes, instinctual and uncontrollable. Stinging with a pre-verbal panic, accompanied by a committee of men with furrowed brows informing me that I wasn't up for this. That writing a check this large was something only "bigger, bolder" people did. Not me.

I didn't share any of this, of course. I'm pretty sure an operations director doesn't want to witness the founder of the company drown in a shallow puddle of her own drama. So I signed the checks. He exited my office, leaving me alone presumably to throw my head back, pump my fists, and laugh like only high-power executive females can do.

In Paulo Coelho's perennial best seller, *The Alchemist*, the hero is a shepherd boy who sets off for an adventure, leaving everything behind and moving toward a bigger calling. Each time he hits an obstacle, a panic, a fear, a deception, he contemplates going backward. Back to where he was more comfortable. Back to his small flock of sheep, sleeping under the stars. Back to simpler times, when he knew what success meant and how it felt.

In that instant, all I wanted was my small flock of sheep. I missed my sheep. I missed the days when I didn't pay taxes because I'd only broken even that year. I missed my first accountant, who had brown front teeth, played bass in a Led Zeppelin tribute band, and smoked with such reckless abandon that a perpetual gray haze hovered around us as we talked more about music than money in the confines of his wood-paneled office walls.

I even missed my Super 8 VIP card.

These days, I had a crisp, shiny accountant who had a sparkly, clean office, a full set of white teeth, and wouldn't know "The Immigrant Song" unless Taylor Swift happened to cover it. I led a team of nine people. And I just spent "a quarter-million bucks!" in a matter of twenty-one seconds.

The thing is, that shepherd boy never did end up going back to his small flock of sheep. He couldn't. That's not the way life (or business) works.

If you're expanding and succeeding in any way, you're always meeting new, challenging situations. New territories. New growth. New trials. And just like the shepherd boy, the calling continues. You expand to answer it, even when it's uncomfortable.

Which is exactly what I did. As the chief interpretation officer—the CIO—of my business, with my interpretation muscle well toned by years of Sunday Summits, I answered the moment. I upleveled. And I became a person who signs checks totaling $269,000.

The CIO is not a storyteller. The CIO is not the nostalgic one who longs for simpler times. The CIO seeks insight, not comfort.

So how you interpret your experiences has real power. It can work for you or against you. When you condition yourself to interpret from a higher plane, your experiences (good and bad) become a fountain of wisdom, not an added anxiety. Your interpretations become your principal navigation tool, leading you and your business to the edges of your expansion.

As I allowed the moment to sink in, I looked out the window at the buds forming on the bare trees and smiled quietly. I said aloud to this expanded me, "Onward."

18

INTERPRETATION TRAPS

There's one key thing to consider when a challenging experience first occurs: which way you move. Typically, our reaction goes in one of two directions.

It can be a *pull*. "I can't let this go. I must hold on."

Or it can be a *push*. "I hate this. Get this out of here."

You either clutch and cling. Or you shove and avoid. And yes, you could argue that these are normal movements. It's survival. It's how we're wired. It's what everyone does.

As an entrepreneur, you're different. (You know that by now, don't you?) And your job is to ask if this conditioned "normal" movement of pulling or pushing serves you and your intention, or if it keeps you stuck. Is it getting in the way of your expansion and ultimately blocking your best decisions and actions?

Interpretation is tricky territory. It's easy to get trapped in fear. As with all elements of the Soul Track, awareness is everything. So the following are a few of the most common traps to watch out for.

INTERPRETATION TRAP #1: THE "ARE YOU SURE?" FACTOR

Sometimes when we set an intention—especially a big, game-changing intention—an odd sort of obstacle can appear. But it won't look like an obstacle at all. In fact, it will often be bright and shiny. It'll appear as a cool opportunity.

Remember that scene in *It's a Wonderful Life* when the evil Mr. Potter brings George Bailey to his office and woos him with cigars and promises of great fortunes? For a brief moment, George Bailey forgets who he is and what he stands for. Until he snaps out of it. When the trance is broken, he runs away from deceit and the easy way out of his troubles.

I call it the "Are you sure?" factor. It's like the universe is checking to see exactly how clear you are in this intention of yours.

Just two days before I was ready to quit my PR job to become a song-writer (and take my jaunt around the world), my boss at Ogilvy & Mather called me to his office and gave me a promotion. *Huh?*

Yes, in the blink of an eye, I could return my backpack and maps and enter the track to a higher-paying position doing much more important work in the PR world of Washington, DC. The grown-ups would swoon. My uncertainty would vanish. More money? A better title? *Toss me that cigar there, Mr. Potter! I don't need my soul anyway!*

Sometimes, when we've gotten clear on what we want, or we've started off in a new direction, a bit of ego porn may tempt us. Our more rational, non-entrepreneurial peers will say, "Well, obviously, go for the sure thing," or, "Well, shit—that's a pretty good offer. I'd take that." And you, the entrepreneur, have to interpret the experience, asking, *Is this calling me to consider an entirely different path? Or to commit more deeply to my intention?* The answer, the interpretation, is never easy.

INTERPRETATION TRAP #2: THE BLAME OF ATTRACTION

Has one of your more "positive" friends ever interpreted your situation by suggesting that you "attracted" it to yourself?

More important, have you ever once found this helpful?

Me either.

And not just because such a sentiment makes you feel like shit. It's because attraction is so passive. Like, there you were. Just being you. And then, unwittingly, you *drew* this horrible experience to yourself. As though, if you were clean, you would only ever attract clean people and clean experiences. There would be no challenges.

This, my friends, is a shame spiral poised at the ready. And not even sort of helpful as you interpret a situation. Please stop using attraction in this way.

Consider instead that you called this situation to you. And you, yourself, say, "This is what I most need for my expansion."

In other words, you *orchestrated* this.

Let's go back to Pam as she was working to transform her Statue of Liberty business model. If she'd turned to one of those Law of Attraction types for help, she might have heard, "Wow. You've got some real issues if you attracted these deceitful people into your life." Pam would then be left searching for her deceitful vibes and unclean energy. She might even end up saying, "I knew it. My energy is bad. This'll never work!"

How does this serve her? It doesn't.

But Pam owned that she orchestrated her situation. That she herself had set an intention to grow her business. So she was able to interpret it differently. *Wow, check it out. I set that intention and what was out of alignment came right to the surface.* With that interpretation she not only avoided the Blame of Attraction Trap, she got clear about the next steps to creating her intention.

INTERPRETATION TRAP #3: THE PRINCIPLE OF THE THING

When I bought the 3,500-square-foot space that became Uplevel World Headquarters, it took almost a year to get the upfit completed. Two weeks after my team finally moved in, I got a 7 AM call from my contractor. A water pipe had burst upstairs, and for fourteen straight hours, hot water had dumped all over our offices, destroying everything. Apparently, the plumber had chosen a cheap shortcut for a mechanism on some of the pipes.

The plumber was busted. The insurance company covered the physical damage. But they refused to cover loss of business for the six months we were forced out of our offices, even though it was part of the policy—right there in black-and-white.

When our lawyer relayed this news to me, I went into a slight rage. And by slight, I mean huge. Six months of inconvenience, running all over town trying to hold meetings. Endless phone calls and rescheduling. Countless hours explaining our situation to clients and vendors.

Our attorney said we could file a lawsuit. But he added that the insurance company was pretty much banking that we wouldn't do that because lawsuits are all-consuming and costly. And insurance companies have lots of money. Much more money than I had. Besides, he cautioned, we could spend a small fortune only to lose the case and be worse off than when we started.

I was furious. I wanted to attack. I wanted to go all Erin Brockovich on them and show them who was who. In that moment, I didn't care how much it cost in time, money, or headaches. It was the *principle of the thing*.

Ah, yes, the principle of the thing. As honorable as it may sound, in reality, the principle of the thing can catch us by our ankles and drag us down to where we cease any and all forward motion. We're no longer aware of our intention or our energy. We're blinded by the injustice of it all.

And this is where you can get tangled up for months and years, holding on to a place of righteous anger. And you know what? You'd be right. You'd most definitely be right. But at some point, this kind of clinging begs the question, "What is *right* costing me energetically?"

There will be injustices on your business journey. There will be insurance agencies that do exactly what this one did. Employees who steal. Clients who don't pay.

This is not to say you should roll over and take it. Rather, it is to say that you must be the one to interpret it and explore whether you want to give your time and energy over to "the principle of the thing."

INTERPRETATION TRAP #4: THE WHY HOLE

"Why" is weird.

In fact, you might think the reason we interpret anything is to figure out why it happened at all. Or to discover the mistakes we made and then correct them, right?

Well, sort of.

Trying to figure out *why* something happened can also be a sweeping, generalizing, judgment bringer. Less about interpretation and more about holding on to blame. Or even discovering a good reason to give up and head back to the couch for reruns of *Gilmore Girls*.

As such, "why" can be a black hole. That's because "why" looks backward. When we look back, we're not necessarily seeking solutions. We really just want an answer. Preferably one that will satisfy our obsessive mind with its constant need to be right. This alone can kill momentum. As the saying goes, you can't reach your destination by looking in the rearview mirror.

Interpreting experiences is about training your brain to discover solutions, insights, and new perspectives. So, sure, you may find a really good answer to "why." But often, that answer is either something you can't do anything about—or it's a way to beat yourself up, especially if the answer points to some fault of yours.

So before you fall into the Why Hole, consider your motivation for wanting to know why. Make sure you're seeking the expansion, not the punishment.

INTERPRETATION TRAP #5: AVOIDING THE TEDIOUS

Let's say your recent email campaign or launch didn't work. Conversions didn't happen. Only one person purchased your product or services. Hardly anyone opened the emails.

It's tempting to interpret it like this: *It was a bad idea.* Or, *no one would ever want this.* Or, worse, *I suck at this.*

Often, what's really happening is simpler than that. But it's also more tedious. If you look a little harder, get a little clearer, you're likely to find that the problem isn't the idea. Or the product. Or you. What you have in this situation, in the words of uber-marketer Dan Kennedy, is a "marketing problem."

A marketing problem means that you have to get granular. You have to study. You have to find the real cause. Like an issue with your messaging or copy or the way the offer was made. Any number of things could be a contributing factor. So you have to get in there and look around.

But, dang, that's tedious. In some ways, interpreting failure as a problem with the entire idea—or with you—is easier, even though it might *feel* worse. After all, it's too late to fix an entire idea. And, let's face it, it's too late to fix *you*. So there's nothing to be done here. You're off the hook.

Strange as it sounds, the thought of doing something tedious can be so stomach churning that you go for the lazy interpretation, which stops you from doing the thing that makes a business work: experimenting, iterating, trying again, and learning.

INTERPRETATION TRAP #6: AVOIDING ENDINGS

You've probably heard the expression, "What got you here won't get you there." You've probably written it down. Maybe it's a quote you save in Evernote. And sometimes, you spout it off because tidy little quotes like that always sound so good and make you feel so wise.

Until they're happening to you. That's when those four little words, "what got you here," get sticky. Because "what got you here" might just be something you're attached to. Or some*one* you're attached to. Or a strategy that used to work so well.

And that's precisely when you stop interpreting and start clinging.

You don't want to lose anything that's proven helpful. Or lose people. You don't want to hurt people. You don't want to step into uncharted territory. Or feel uncertain. You don't want to give up *what got you here* in order to *get there*.

The trap is that you're conflating completions with abandonment. Or failure. Completions are not endings or abandonments. A completion is simply something that has run its course—and run it so well that the situation is now calling for something new, something different that can take you to the next level.

If business is anything, it's a lifelong lesson in letting go. Upleveling is a lot more about what you release than it is about what you add. As Dr. Henry Cloud says in his book, *Necessary Endings*, "When something *ends* in a business, it doesn't mean you're doing something wrong, it means you're still alive."

INTERPRETATION TRAP #7: THE SPIRITUAL BYPASS

The trickiest and stickiest interpretation trap happens when an entrepreneur has decided to be "spiritual." And from this lofty plane, that entrepreneur avoids facing the reality of an experience head-on.

Yes, it's great that so many spiritual principles and practices are now mainstream. But when it comes to interpretation, our clamoring little egos love to co-opt a good spiritual principle and use it to deflect the necessity of taking uncomfortable action. It's tempting to hide behind spirituality, to pretend we're above earthly conflicts. It's convenient, and, best of all, we get to feel slightly superior while doing it.

But, uh-oh, you have a business. And in any business, especially when it's growing, some truly wacked-out, earthly shit can happen. False accusations, broken contracts, injustices, betrayals. It's like public high school on steroids. As such, it can bring up the inner reactions you most don't want to see or want anyone else to see either.

So the "spiritual" person finds an out. She gets to use spirituality as a way to avoid what feels too ugly to face.

Mia is an acupuncturist. She developed several herbal-healing formulas and found a partner to help her start up an e-commerce site to sell them worldwide. But her partner ended up stealing the formulas and keeping the money Mia had invested.

As someone who teaches and encourages practices like meditation and Qigong, Mia was now in wildly unfamiliar territory. Fury was her new friend. Anger seemed to own her. And more than ever, with her savings drained, she had to keep her practice going, even while the hot energy of rage consumed her. She hated the feeling. She wanted it gone.

Then she heard about a prayer called Ho'oponopono—a Hawaiian practice where a mantra is used to create forgiveness and right action. The prayer—and all the stories of people using it—seemed miraculous. And so, wanting to be free of the rage, she recited the prayer fervently.

Weeks went by, and it wasn't working. Her ex-partner wasn't doing the right thing: namely, giving Mia her money back and realizing he was an idiot. And Mia was still furious. When she finally shared all of this with me, she wanted to know what she was doing wrong.

After talking through the details, I asked her if she'd considered hiring an attorney.

She said, "I wanted to avoid that stuff. That seems so corporate or something."

Mia was doing what spiritual people are "supposed" to do. Spiritual people are supposed to be nice, to not have lawyers, to trust in the process, never get angry, and roll with everything as the will of the Universe. And then to use prayers and energy work to help them transcend it. (And make the idiots in the world do the right thing.)

Adding weight to her choice, Mia had heard my story about the insurance company and my decision not to get legal—more proof she was doing the right thing.

But there's a key difference. And that is the motivation behind my choice. That motivation was different from Mia's motivation. I had worked through the rage. From a place of clarity, I was able to interpret my circumstance in a way that led to the conclusion not to take further legal action.

Mia was using the bullet points of my situation in an effort to avoid her own. And then propping the whole thing up with a prayer she hoped would rectify everything without having to confront anyone.

This interpretation trap is called the Spiritual Bypass. I told Mia that you can bet you've taken that bypass if you're reciting a prayer and then whipping your head around to see if it "worked." Like, if you've attached a spiritual practice to a specific outcome, thereby treating it more like a magic trick. What Mia was trying to sidestep was the discomfort of admitting that something had gone legally astray here, as well as the practical steps involved with making it right.

"But I don't want to stoop to his level," she said. "It feels like I've given up, and I'm mucking in the worst parts of business."

"You *are* in business, Mia," I pointed out. "And this is part of being on the Strategy Track and the Soul Track simultaneously. You're moving in all worlds at once. And you have a choice in front of you here: You can recite that mantra and hope for the best. Or you can recite the mantra, use it as a way to align yourself, while also allowing an attorney to help you get your money and formulas back, and possibly get some therapy to help you process your anger. This is real stuff here. You may need to face it in order to resolve it."

It took a year and a lot of practice and focus, but Mia finally embraced a different interpretation: She realized she had indeed been hiding. She let the situation call her to stand up for herself, something she'd never been good at. She took on the work while remaining connected to spirit.

In the end, Mia got her money back. She and her attorney had to negotiate for the formulas, as they were not patented. But most importantly, she grew from her clear interpretation and the experiences it led to. She gained skills in navigating the legal system. She set up structures to protect her finances and her formulas. She also learned that sometimes the "will of the universe" is to take practical action—and that confrontation can be the more spiritual choice.

Becoming a skillful interpreter means being willing to be still and stay with an experience, much like Mia learned. That stillness makes room for awareness. And within that awareness is clarity. This is how you build trust in yourself and become a wise and skillful business owner. Getting caught in interpretation traps is normal. It's going to happen. But being able to recognize when you're in a trap, know how to extricate yourself, and return to awareness is extraordinary and worth celebrating. It means you know *your* interpretation is *yours* to choose. And under those rules, it's within your power to *always* choose interpretations that advance your intentions and expand your life and business.

NAVIGATING DECISIONS

19

THE PLAY-BIG ZONE

I t was late afternoon in Tucson, which meant it was about 103 degrees outside. But standing at the front of the air-conditioned meeting room, I was shivering. As I watched the ten women file out for a bathroom break before our final session, my mind replayed a recent story I'd heard about a client mutiny.

One of my peers had started a mastermind. At the first roundtable meeting, her clients turned on her. First, they colluded. Then they got aggressive. Before she knew it, they were accusing her of being a fraud and demanding their money back. One by one, her clients walked out of the retreat, never to return.

In the now-empty conference room, I wondered if I was in the same tenuous territory. This wasn't a mutiny exactly. But something was definitely not working.

I was coaching my first yearlong group mastermind. This was our second retreat, and we were moving into the zone of decision-making. A critical—and to me, pretty exciting—part of business. Yet the energy in the room was sluggish all day. Skepticism reigned.

Anyone who has ever taught anything or led any kind of group knows that groups have energy. No single workshop or retreat is ever the same workshop or retreat—even if the content is the same. The energy of the group is the X factor. It's where momentum is created or totally dies. Great teachers, performers, and yes, coaches learn how and when to ride, elevate, or shift that energy as needed. But I was now discovering that teaching is a radically different experience from my years on stage as an entertainer and musician.

As each woman got up in front of the room for her session, a heaviness, a fatigue, set in. I taught strategies, and they were met with doubt. I offered ideas, but they were smashed down. When I added up the numbers for one consultant's launch, she rolled her eyes and said, "Like *I'm* going to make that happen." When I encouraged an herbalist to pay herself a salary instead of waiting to see if there was money left at the end of each month, she looked out the window and bit her nails. Each person seemed to be wearing her own secret Wonder Woman cuffs. Only instead of deflecting harm, these bracelets were deflecting possibility.

It was a mutiny of "meh."

During the final session of the day, my own energy had vanished. I had caught the doubt virus that was going around. I was questioning my abilities as a coach. I wasn't inspiring these rookie business owners. They couldn't see how their choices drove their success. Even when a few of them saw an opening and began making decisions about next moves, their enthusiasm was squelched by the others who kept turning the collective attention to the things that didn't work, and all the reasons they *wouldn't* work.

When the session closed, we all went to dinner together. Suddenly, everybody was upbeat. They joked. They drank wine. They poked fun at the intensity of my coaching methods, laughing at the moments when I had called someone out about something.

They weren't taking any of it seriously. And their laughter felt fake. It was like a heavy veil was keeping everyone outwardly jovial and cheerfully bonded in their doubts, their nondecisions, and their inaction. By the time dinner ended, I felt sad and drained.

When I got back to my room, I sank into the chair by my desk. *What the fuck?* I thought, staring at the wall for several minutes. Rather than wandering down the moping rabbit hole I knew so well, I decided to get curious instead. I sat still and breathed, tuning in to the energy of the day and my own intentions as a coach.

On one hand, I was frustrated at their behavior. On the other hand, I empathized. Decisions are scary. They require clarity and a level of trust most of us were not taught. So many doubts arise from so many arenas—our personal history, our peers, not to mention a world that's more drawn to the cynical and sarcastic than to the power of intention and clarity.

As if on cue, a memory appeared. A moment from my past when I discovered that I myself had committed to doubt more than to decision.

THE CHANCE TO DRAW BACK

It all started when I'd shared my music dreams with Jim, a grad school friend of my big brother's. I hadn't told anyone in my family yet, and Jim was underwhelmed by my vision, saying, "You really think you have a chance in hell to make it?" When I said I didn't know, he shrugged. Then he said, "Well, try it for a year. And if you don't make it . . . give it up and get a job."

I was twenty-three at the time. Jim was thirty-one. Which meant he was old. And I figured old people were wise. So I thought this was solid advice.

Until one fateful evening when I was well past a year in my attempt to be a musician. I had taken steps, yes. I had recovered from my South Africa breakup. I had moved. I was waitressing, writing songs, and practicing music. But by anyone's standards, I had certainly not "made it."

I was living in an apartment above a dry cleaner, driving a fifteen-year-old Datson 310. I hadn't even done my first open mic night. For the hundredth day in a row, I was debating whether it was time to call it quits. Just home from the dinner shift, I sat down hard on my wood floor, tip money falling out of my pockets. I sighed and opened a book a friend had just loaned me. And I stumbled on a passage that took my breath away:

Until one is committed, there is hesitancy, the chance to draw back, always ineffectiveness. Concerning all acts of initiative (and creation), there is one elementary truth, the ignorance of which kills countless ideas and splendid plans. That the moment one definitely commits oneself, then providence moves, too. All sorts of things occur to help one that would never otherwise have occurred.

The man who wrote this—almost a half-century earlier—was a mountain climber, an adventurer named W. H. Murray. I read his words about ten times. Then I read the first sentence ten times more. I thought of how, every single day, I gave myself "the chance to draw back." I made excuses. I found reasons I wasn't good enough, always looking to the outside world to make my decisions for me. I rarely told anyone I was working on a music career. I wouldn't put the full force of my own spirit behind this thing I wanted to do. That way, I reasoned, if I failed, no one would ever know.

And there it was on the page. I hadn't committed. I hadn't tapped into what could be called the most powerful energy available to us as humans: decision. Instead, I dabbled. I whined. I waited for someone to see all this potential I had and perhaps make my decisions for me.

Then this strange man, W. H. Murray, stepped into my apartment—returning to the planet decades after he uttered those words—to grab me by the shoulders and tell me I hadn't even begun my climb. That, at best, I was dipping my toe in the water and wimping out because it was cold. And that it was time to get real. To commit and make decisions that would manifest my intention.

I ripped a piece of paper from my journal, wrote his words on it, and posted it on the wall of my music room.

DREAMS REQUIRE DECISIONS, DECISIONS REQUIRE COMMITMENT

If I had to pick one thing that changed my career as a musician, that would be the moment that did it. Not because angels sang, or some molecular collision happened and the way became clear, or because Quincy Jones himself finally found out that there was this undiscovered, mildly talented twenty-four-year-old with all kinds of potential living above the Dun Kwik Cleaners in Swannanoa, North Carolina. It was because I gave up Jim's "try it for a year" plan. It was because I stopped dipping my toe in.

Using the power of commitment, I started making and acting on decisions despite the external and internal "nos" I faced each day. I shared my dream with others. I did my first open mic. I got my first gig. I started making my first CD in the basement of another musician's house, saving my tip money to pay him for the sessions. I stopped waiting for things to happen and started deciding.

And now, in my hotel room in Tucson, I saw clearly. Commitment was what my clients needed, too. Sure, they'd set their intentions for their businesses. They'd taken the step of investing in themselves by being at this mastermind. But when it came right down to it, they weren't making decisions. They weren't committed. They were counting on me to drag them across that line. They wanted me to believe in them for them. But that's not something I—or any coach or other person—can do. They needed to find that commitment within themselves.

And that was something I *could* help them with.

So, in my bare feet, wearing only my bathrobe, while the rest of the hotel slept, I padded down to the conference room where our table and materials were still set up for our second day of coaching and masterminding. I grabbed a poster board and created a big sign using colorful markers and as much style as I could muster at one in the morning.

This might not work, I thought. *But then again, it might.*

The next morning when my clients arrived, the door to the conference room was closed. I was inside. But rather than walking right in, chatting, and getting their coffees in the usual fashion, they were stopped by a challenge. A big sign on the door read:

**You are entering an
OFFICIAL PLAY-BIG ZONE
The following is PROHIBITED:**

- Sarcasm, whining, complaining
- Blaming anyone (or anything) for your results
- Distracting/self-deprecating humor
- Being a victim

The following is REQUIRED!

- Taking full responsibility for your life and your results
- Claiming the powerful woman you are
- Recognizing that your clarity makes you UNSTOPPABLE
- DECIDING to live from your highest, clearest whole self
- BECOMING the person you are destined to be
- Full engagement (No checking out!)

**THIS IS NOT A JOKE.
Take one moment. Get still inside. Be clear & powerful.
Then (and only then) STEP INSIDE . . .**

I could hear their chatter at first. Then, nothing. Dead silence. I thought maybe they'd each read the sign and left, going back to breakfast where things were more fun. Mutiny.

But then the door opened, and one woman walked in and sat down. Then the next. Then the next. Soon, there were eleven of us around the table looking at each other. Two people had tears on their cheeks. But everyone was present: clear and determined.

Right there, before my eyes, they had committed. Supported by the power of that commitment, they made their first set of decisions: to walk through that door and take on the opportunities this mastermind presented to them.

"Ready to get started?" I asked. They all nodded.

As we went about our second day of work together, everything shifted. Now energized and strengthened by commitment, they made themselves vulnerable, faced the unknown, explored possibilities, took responsibility, and, yes, made decisions.

Some of these same clients, people who've gone on to create empires, still occasionally post a photo of my handmade sign in their Facebook feed, crediting this moment as the major turnaround for them.

A DECISION IS INTENTION WITH LEGS

Now you are entering the territory of decision-making. That means big and little decisions. At this point, the first three stages we've walked through in this book might seem fairly manageable. After all, when you initiate your intention, you form your idea and you start executing, making plans, envisioning your future. You can do that, sure. When you manage your power, you observe your old patterns and deal with resistance as it shows up along the way. When you interpret experiences, you view the things that happen with an eye toward your expansion. All of this can be done without too much risk of losing face or fortune. In some ways, these first three stages are internal.

Then comes the moment of decision. And—as the expression goes—shit gets real. You choose a date. You pick a color. You draw the line. You set a deadline. And with that, you're outed. You show the world you're committed to this intention of yours.

The minute you set that deadline and let other people know, it hits you. You become Wile E. Coyote remembering the law of gravity the very second he runs off the cliff after Road Runner. Right before he plummets, leaving only a wisp of smoke behind, his eyes reveal that reality has struck.

For a brief moment, I am Wile E. Coyote every time (and I mean *every* time) my team and I set a date—whether it's for a webinar, an event, a retreat, or a workshop. The decision is made. No more flirting around the edges and dancing with my ideas. The plummet to action must begin now. Down I go.

A decision, I like to tell my clients, is "intention with legs." Commitment gets those legs moving. Decisions are how we begin to execute the ideas in our heads and how those ideas become our reality. Therefore, decisions are intense, personally revealing, and can make you feel vulnerable. But they're also powerful. Through them, you take a forward step. You change the status quo.

COMMITTED, NOT CONVINCED

And now it's time to state the obvious. No decision comes with a guarantee. As much as you may know this at some level, there's a whole other level, a whole other part of us that simply can't get behind this reality.

This is why, when we're faced with a decision, we also face a litany of doubts. Doubt wants proof. Doubt wants pro-and-con lists. Doubt wants to be convinced. Doubt says, "Until I am convinced about this decision, I will ruminate. I will plague you. I will engage you in all kinds of socially acceptable behaviors that keep your energy just slightly outside of this thing."

So here's the thing: "I'm In" is not the same as "I'm convinced." In the entrepreneurial world, "I'm convinced" is child's play. If you insist on being convinced before you make a decision, then you've made little more than an excuse. It's an excuse to stay in a holding pattern, taking half-hearted actions that waste your time and energy. Dipping your toe in. Or "trying it for a year" (à la Jim). As prudent as this might look to the world, it's all just evidence you're still playing games, rehearsing worst-case scenarios, and hosting a tug-of-war in your mind.

Even though your brain contributes to your decision-making process, the energy of commitment, which is bigger, does not reside in your mind. As much as we like to think our funny little mind will figure everything out, it usually does little more than argue back and forth with itself. Commitment, on the other hand, is your whole being. And, as you are about to discover, it's an inconceivably powerful energy.

20

JUST TELL ME WHAT TO DO

Confession: I hate selling. When my clients start working with me, many of them feel the same way. So they're relieved to discover we're bonded on the issue.

But then I disappoint them. Because I also love selling. I love that the sales transaction, more than anything else, brings our stuff to the surface, lays it bare, and forces us to deal with it. While selling can, and often does, use manipulative tactics and ridiculous, pushy language, a sale can also be done with relentless clarity, stellar communication, and detachment.

No matter the approach, selling is ultimately about decision. And decision, by definition, lands us (whether seller or prospect) in the arena of uncertainty. It's uncomfortable.

Being the one selling is an especially vulnerable spot. Rejection looms large. Even more cringeworthy, you become privy to the decision-making process when you (or your service) are the thing being decided upon. In that empty quiet, you witness all the ways someone who was undeniably excited to sign up just minutes before now begins to squirm, trying to avoid the decision.

They tell you their spouse won't let them do it. They say that they'd *totally* do it, but their biggest client just cut back, and the money isn't there. They'll get irritated or angry or make a derisive snorting noise when you reveal your pricing. They'll tell you they need to check their Oracle Cards.

Or someone might grab you by the arm at your own event and accuse you of being the worst salesperson they ever met. Which happened to me. In this scenario, the arm-grabbing accuser was an aesthetician named Peggy. During the event, I'd opened the doors to my yearlong mastermind. And though Peggy wanted to work with me, the investment to sign up wasn't cheap.

So all that stuff that comes up when we're faced with a decision—well, 10× it when money's involved. Even those who are ready to take the leap get terrified. I've seen people crying and sweating as they sign on the dotted line. Those who aren't sure what to do (like Peggy) often express that uncertainty by getting pissed—pissed!—at me for making an offer at all. Some simply freeze.

They're all facing a decision.

And their reactions are about much more than the money. Any decision carries with it a whole host of consequences, internal as well as external. They worry that they don't have the strength or clarity to manage these uncertain elements. *If I choose this, will I fail? Will I hurt someone? If I do this new thing, will I be uncomfortable? Will I end up a bag lady?*

So our egos come to the rescue. And they find all kinds of ways to help us avoid these scary questions and challenges. They find ways for us to avoid making a decision altogether.

A POWERLESS MANTRA

Peggy had already asked me many questions. She'd talked with my clients. She'd grilled my team of coaches several times over. And she still couldn't make a decision.

That's when she grabbed me. I was about to step on stage to teach the final session of the event. She blew back her bangs and looked down at me and said, "Something's wrong here, you know that? Either you're subtly rejecting me or you're the worst salesperson I ever met."

It was meant to sting. And it did. But I took a deep breath and kept quiet as Peggy continued, "I mean, you're not even trying all that hard to get me to be your client here. I'm asking you to tell me what to do!"

There are times when someone is simply scared to believe in themselves. In such cases, "closing a sale" is a matter of taking their hand and guiding them over that line. So you help them do that. Sure, you can use the strategies you've learned from Zig or Cialdini. Or even the late and legendary Dan Kennedy, who, in this case, would probably say that Peggy's gonna spend her money somewhere, so it might as well be with me. So close the sale and be done with it, right?

Yeah. Okay. Sometimes I can do that.

But the right phrasing and cool tactics can also be a disservice to someone. And from what Peggy had told me, she had been closed, sold, converted, and pushed into so many programs out there that she needed something different this time. She needed to change how she made decisions. Namely, she needed to actually make one. On her own. Without me being yet another person who just tells her what to do.

I hear it all the time. Sometimes from clients who are confused about a strategy. Sometimes from potential clients, like Peggy. "Just tell me what to do." We've all made that request of a mentor, parent, partner, or friend. In fact, the terrain of business coaching is littered with exhausted entrepreneurs who were told "what to do."

It's just easier, right? Easier to be told what to do. And easier to tell people what to do. Working through the complexities of our own insides is hard. It hurts. And whatever we choose is on us. That's a lot of responsibility. So handing the reins to someone else is a relief. But only in the moment.

That's because, in the long run, "just tell me what to do" is a powerless mantra. As with intention, power, and interpretation, whenever we look to someone or something outside ourselves to make our decisions, we walk out on our business. We shrink ourselves, our role, and our ownership. We withdraw our spirit from that arena. And your decision is going to need your spirit if it's going to do its best for your business.

So I signaled to the AV team to keep the music rolling. I chose to delay the module so I could sit down with Peggy one last time.

"Peggy," I said, "this is not rejection. I think this mastermind could be a great experience for you. You've seen for yourself the high value of our content and high touch of our coaches. But if I tell you what to do, I rob you. If you look around at the people who have signed up, some are terrified. Some are crying. They're having hard conversations with spouses. They're uncomfortable. But this is a powerful part of the process. As much as I want to fix it and make it not be hard or promise them a million bucks tomorrow, I don't. Maybe that makes me a terrible salesperson. But I won't tell them—or you—what to do. I don't want to remove the internal growth and confidence that comes from deciding yes or no for yourself."

Her face sank.

Then she got up. As she walked away, she turned around and told me that I just lost myself a "pretty damn good client."

At least she made a decision.

THE ONE-WORD WISDOM KILLER

Back when I was a musician on the road somewhere in the Midwest, I was up late one night in my hotel room. I caught an MTV video that featured an electric guitar player in a vast wheat field surrounded by a cadre of women clad in nothing but plastic thongs. I got a great idea for a song.

The next day, it no longer felt like a great idea. So I called my friend Kathy. I explained about the video and my song idea—and shared a list of reasons my idea was boring. Then I asked her if I should just give up on the idea—and, while I was at it, if I should give up on everything else, too? (I tossed in that extra part just in case.)

After a long pause, Kathy said, "Tell you what, Christine. You write the song. Then we'll decide if it's good."

Kathy smashed my *should* to pieces and then handed the decision back to me.

You already know this from the last chapter but it bears repeating: There's absolutely *no* way to know if a decision to do something is going to work out until you do it. In fact, there may be ten good reasons it's *not* going to work. "Should" has no bearing on any of it.

As a coach, when I hear the word "should," I see a big red flag. It's one more way to get someone to tell you what to do. "Should I have speakers at my event?" Or "Should I hire a project manager?" Or "Should I start a podcast?" When a client starts a question with that word, I know that something—responsibility, action, clarity, power—is being avoided.

The answer to "Should I?" is not a yes or no. (Though way too many business coaches feel the pressure to have quick, easy answers, so they rely on their opinions about speakers at events, hiring project managers, or starting podcasts.) "Should" is often just procrastination by inquiry. As in, "Should I write this song?" Tossing "should" into the decision-making mix is also a convenient and socially acceptable way to shut down a deeper exploration of the issues at hand, killing off real wisdom.

THE TWO-WORD WISDOM BRINGER

More often than not, the best answer to "Should I?" is "It depends."

"It depends" guides the navigation. It requires us to dig a little deeper to understand the situation and the parameters involved. On the surface, that sucks because it's so much easier to fire off a quick answer and be done with it. "Yes, you should! You absolutely should! Next caller please!" But in reality, "It depends" is the only way for us to get to the best decision.

If we're facing the truth here—and we are—"should" is nothing more than "tell me what to do" in disguise. It's just another attempt to get the go-ahead from someone or something outside ourselves. Another way to avoid the decision. This is not to say that we never ask others for their thoughts, experiences, or opinions when making a decision. But what matters here is the energy we bring to the table when we ask for that input.

It pays to look at how you ask. Let's say you're struggling with a decision. And say you're sharing that struggle with a friend. You tell her the direction you're thinking of taking. And then you add some kind of typical self-deprecating finisher, like ". . . or is that the stupidest thing you've ever heard?" (As I did in not so many words with Kathy.)

The person you've asked, rather than being able to focus on your decision, now has to deal with the question you've presented: Is that the stupidest thing they've ever heard? Which is dramatic, negative, and has nothing at all to do with the options you're trying to sort through.

When it comes to asking for other people's input, your energy must be clear and your motive one of perspective gathering versus looking for a way out. If your energy is tentative (*Should I?*), dismissive (*I would suck at that, right?*), or outright avoidant (*Tell me what to do!*), the person you're asking is now dealing with your energy and trying to fulfill that need. They may not be able to articulate it, but in the absence of *your* clarity, they'll give you *theirs*, tossing their opinions into the mix, often without considering you or your intention or context.

By the way, I did indeed write that song. It was called "No Such Thing as Girls Like That," and it became hands down the most popular song at my shows.

THE DECISION FILTER: BUILDING YOUR DECISION PROCESS

The truth is, with any decision you face, you know your context and intention better than anyone. Sure, there are people with more certifications, more experience in your field, and bigger bottom lines. But when it comes to your business, you bring the real wisdom to the table. You are the wise thinker. To make decisions that advance your intention, it helps to see yourself that way. You need to allow your wisdom to be the main driver of your decisions—no matter how many opinions you solicit.

That's hard. I know. So to help my clients get there, I developed a tool called "the Decision Filter." It's a series of questions that guides you through the context of your decision (the "it depends" territory). The following questions allow you to explore your options and consider the various parameters involved.

1. What is my intention for my business?

Knowing where you want to go informs your choices. Everything starts with setting your intention and remaining true to it. Get clear and anchor to it by writing it out.

2. What is this decision I'm considering?

Again, this is about clarity. Write down the components of this decision without worrying about perfect prose. Sometimes my clients will find they've actually covered up the key decision they need to make with all kinds of ideas and directions, confusing themselves even more.

3. How might the results of this decision contribute to my intention?

This is where you ensure this decision you're weighing is aligned with the intention for your business. For instance, let's say your intention is to have ten clients in your top-tier package. A decision to redesign your website right now might not align with that intention—unless you could prove that doing so would have a direct impact on getting those clients.

4. What is the biggest challenge I'm having in my business right now? Is this decision related to that challenge?

This will help you see whether or not you're getting distracted by another bright, shiny object (i.e., a pretty new website) or truly solving the challenges at hand.

5. How might the results of this decision solve my biggest challenge?

If this decision isn't about your biggest challenge, ask yourself if it's worth taking on a new option when there are other, more pressing things that haven't been faced yet.

6. How might this decision be a distraction from my biggest challenge?

For those who like to avoid things that are tedious—like current challenges—this is a good question to consider.

7. If I consider my current business metrics (list size, team size, bandwidth), how does this decision match those metrics? Is the timing right when I examine these numbers?

The timing of decisions is crucial. Many things we want to do are great ideas, but they aren't aligned with the current numbers in our business and will often lead us into overwhelm and down new rabbit holes.

8. What do I need to consider in terms of bandwidth—my time, my team's time—when it comes to the impact this decision might have?

Okay, sure, this question's a bummer for those who only want to be excited about new possibilities and directions—but think about whether you have the time and energy to take on this new direction.

9. Why am I considering this now? Why right now and not later?

This is one of the questions I ask clients. I want to encourage them to have ideas. After all, that's what builds their business. But sometimes a little bit of perspective on the driver behind a decision can open up a deeper motivation that may not be serving the entrepreneur.

And your bonus question:

10. What do I know that I'm pretending not to know?

This epic question calls forth wisdom that's often hanging out in the darkness, waiting for a light to shine on it. See what comes up when you pose this question. It may be that nothing surfaces. If there's nothing, then let it go and see if anything reveals itself as you go about your day. Sometimes, an instant insight will arise.

The Decision Filter process helps you access your wisdom—what you know, feel, intuit—allowing that to become the foundation of your decision-making choices. So if you elect to gather more information, ask for advice, or turn to your coach, you do so with your own substantial understanding and perspective on the situation. Thus, you have better, more pointed questions to ask. You can be more engaged in discussions and weighing options. In the end, whatever decision you make, it'll be better. And, most important, it'll be yours.

To download a supremely cool printable copy of The Decision Filter and other tools in this book, visit www.SoulSourcedBook.com.

DECISIONS AND DISAPPROVAL

When you get stronger in your decision-making as a business owner, you don't always get buy-in from everyone around you. Your family, your partner, your friends might not approve. They may even express disappointment. If you're used to making sure everyone around you is happy and approves of you, you may discover that you're being called into a new kind of strength and clarity.

My client Carrie Frye is a writing coach and novelist. After taking part in several of Uplevel's online trainings, she came to one of our three-day events and realized she wanted to sign up for the mastermind, though the size of the investment scared her. She went home that evening and talked it through with her husband. Looking at their budget and looking at what her business was currently bringing in, they both agreed it was too much money at the time and too much risk.

Then Carrie woke up in the middle of the night, knowing she had to make this investment in herself. When she told her husband the news in the morning, he wasn't happy. He did not talk to her for days. These days, she humorously describes that scene as "chilly" around the house.

Making decisions can mean loving people enough to let them be disappointed in the decisions you make. Deciding for yourself means confronting your truth, your fears, and perhaps even silence from your spouse. But in that confronting and truth finding—and not avoiding—we find, grow, and strengthen our wisdom about our business. Always.

Within three months of joining the mastermind, Carrie had created a new package, offered it to a select list of clients, and gained the wherewithal to charge a fee reflective of its benefit. Their response more than doubled her income for the year—and paid for the mastermind several times over. She went on to make six figures that year, a number that was four times more than she had ever generated. Since then, her business and her income have only expanded. And needless to say, her husband's trust in her decision-making prowess has expanded as well. So has hers.

MAGIC AND THE
SINGLE STREAM OF INCOME

GMA Studios, Raleigh, North Carolina, 3:30 PM

"Oh it's perfect! It's *perfect!*" said Louise, as she stared at the necklace. Then, as the fourth stone—the emerald—caught her eye, she burst into tears.

Ginger Meek Allen wasn't unfamiliar with this kind of reaction when a client saw their custom-made piece of jewelry for the first time. Still, her eyes filled with tears, too. When Ginger designed this piece, she considered all the details Louise had shared about her life. So she included gems to symbolize not just Louise's three living children, but also Louise's son, who had died in Afghanistan a year earlier.

The piece was a talisman of sorts. Its purpose was to celebrate Louise's sixtieth birthday, honor her life as a mom and wife, and remind her of the creativity and healing the coming years would embody. People often sought out Ginger to create a piece of jewelry to empower an intention as they entered a new beginning in their lives.

Ginger watched as Louise stared at the necklace, taking in its emotion, intention, and energy. *This is my* why. *It was never about the bling. It's about the story. It's about adorning yourself with spirit.* She stayed present with Louise, feeling a sense of awe, not just in the creation of this piece, but also in the decisions she had been courageous enough to make to re-create her business.

Only two years prior, Ginger was living out the results of heeding the warnings of business strategists, believing they knew more than she did about her own jewelry-design business.

She'd always made room for mystery and magic in her work. But once she'd set the intention to start this business in earnest, mystery and magic had taken a back seat to fear. So she looked to the practical advice of several business consultants to relieve that fear. Even though their advice often left her feeling small and unsure, she adhered to their message: "You wanna be an artist? Okay then. Set up multiple streams of income, plan on teaching art, or else you'll be broke."

So she scrambled to create the multiple income streams they recommended. Dutifully, she rented out benches in the studio space she owned. Every day, local metalsmiths entered her sacred space. They'd casually ask her questions, want guidance, and they'd get it. For free.

Ginger also turned a segment of her space into a retail location to sell what she, her renters, and an assortment of other local artists produced. But that meant more interruptions as she, the owner, stopped her own work to sell everybody else's pieces.

She was supposed to be grateful for the customers and sales, but more often she found herself resentful and too distracted to get her own work done. As she scrambled to keep up with all these income streams, the magic that had been the hallmark of her work was left withering—neglected and unfed—on her studio floor.

Then, at the end of a year of scant revenue and even less profit, she asked herself: *What am I doing? And why? What do I really want here?* The answer came loud and clear: To build GMA Designs and focus solely on her work as a custom jewelry designer.

That's when Ginger realigned with her intention. She gathered her energy. And she started making decisions. Her own decisions. Decisions that supported her intention.

She closed down the studio-space rentals. She stopped being a retailer, turning the entire space into her own studio, private showroom, and consultation space. She communicated that she would only be operating as a custom-design metalsmith. And she tripled her pricing.

When her first custom order came in, the client didn't bat an eye at Ginger's new rates. And with all the space she finally had, she started developing an impeccable system that made the process a breeze, even when customers began calling from around the world.

Word got around and more orders came in. Ginger raised her prices again, and she hired an assistant to help with streamlining the process. She was then able to get more work done. The voices of all the business strategists were still in her head: She'd go broke. She'd end up a starving artist. But they weren't driving her business or making her decisions any longer.

In one year, Ginger's income went up 37 percent, even without all of those other income streams! These days, her commission orders have a wait list. She began a signature line on her own website, and now GMA is in more than fifty galleries, boutiques, and museum stores around the country, including the revered Georgia O'Keeffe Museum.

As she watched Louise place her necklace in the GMA signature box, Ginger knew the best part of all: that having a successful business as an artist wasn't about trading in the magic for the money. You could have both. The proof was all around her. In Louise's eyes, in the necklace Ginger had created, and even in the metal dust that sparkled in the afternoon sun on her studio floor.

21

THIS IS YOUR BRAIN
ON DECISIONS

'm exhausted and everything sucks."

This was Charisse's greeting as she picked up the phone for our coaching call. She was weeks away from hosting a two-day event, and she and her assistant Alex were steeped in last-minute details.

I laughed. "Sucking" wasn't Charisse's usual stance, so I asked her to elaborate.

"Well, maybe this'll give you an idea," she said as I heard a rhythmic thwacking sound on the other end of the line. "Hear that? It's an empty Pringles can. Empty! And not the cute little cans you get at the checkout. This was a tall one. We're talking the jumbo family picnic size. I ate the whole thing. And know what else? I haven't even looked at my slides. I haven't written emails I need to write. I tried straightening up my desk. Filing papers. Not gonna happen. So it was 'Hello Pringles.' And I've been ignoring Alex and all her emails since Monday."

When a client hits this state, a business coach might review the list of to-dos and help her get back on course. But this wasn't a place I'd seen Charisse go before, so I decided to press pause and go deeper.

"How about this, Charisse? Tell me about the event plans and where things are right now. And I promise not to confiscate your Pringles."

"Nothing left to confiscate," Charisse laughed. "But okay." Then she launched into a sentence that lasted for about four minutes and had little, if any, punctuation:

"You know how events are, right? You have, like, a hundred and fifty people all wanting different things and writing in with questions. And in the meantime you're trying to figure out stuff like name tags and coffee breaks. And Alex keeps pinging me with new questions and new decisions—like lunch. Lunch! They have this buffet at the hotel, and I'm supposed to decide if I'm paying for lunch on the second day or if they buy their own lunch and if so, how I let them know this—and I can't figure out how to budget if you've never done an event before and I'm at the point I can't even *look* at a number, you know? Oh, and add to that the small issue of the print deadline . . . so I told Alex I'd get back to her about lunch later. And guess what? I still haven't! And by now, I wouldn't be surprised if she quit or something."

Bingo.

Charisse continued her tirade. But the logjam had made itself clear, and it was lunch.

Lunch had stopped Charisse in her tracks. Not lunch exactly. But the unmade decision about the buffet, buried among weeks of nonstop decisions.

If you and I were to geek out on brain science, here's how we'd see this: We'd point to the area right behind our forehead. We'd say, "Ah, yes. The prefrontal cortex."

The official types will tell you that the prefrontal cortex is the center of "executive functioning." In less yawn-worthy lingo, this just means that when presented with a decision, your prefrontal cortex goes to work rounding up relevant information—pertinent facts, related experiences, feelings you have, and even consequences. After that, its job is to examine the data from various points of view. It plays out different scenarios and weighs options.

All of this takes energy. Lots of it. It's why you feel physically exhausted after a morning of tackling issues at your desk—though you never once got up from your chair. It's called Decision Fatigue. It also explains why, when you let a decision go unmade, it's like propping a metaphoric car on cinder blocks, tossing a brick on the gas pedal, and letting the engine just run and run. It leaves you feeling incapable and pooped. The prefrontal cortex just keeps spinning in the background, but no destination is reached.

Worse, the prefrontal cortex doesn't stop working until a decision is made. So when a decision's left tooling around in your head, your brain is still motoring away, demanding fuel.

Sometimes you need to delay a choice and let the engine idle for a bit. Sleeping on it might be worth it—like when you're deciding on changing program content or making a new hire. But when a decision has relatively minor consequences—say, comping a buffet lunch—allowing it to remain unmade comes at too high a price. Better to make it as quickly as possible, get it out of your prefrontal cortex, and save your energy for more significant tasks, like building the slides for your presentation.

Oh, and one more thing: the prefrontal cortex helps to regulate your behavior, which means when it's functioning well, you naturally grab just a few chips instead of the whole family-size can, which, at this moment, ceased its repetitive tapping in the background as Charisse concluded, "and I still don't know what to do about the buffet!"

I jumped in while I had the chance. "Lightning-round question, Charisse. Ready?" I asked. "If you *did* know, what would you choose?"

"I'd just pay for it," Charisse said. Then there was a pause. "Oh hey, that was easy, wasn't it?"

Decision made. Open loop closed. Energy now available for the next item on the agenda.

MANAGING DECISIONS

One of my favorite Seth Godin blog posts is titled, "What Do You Make?" His readers—we entrepreneurs—oh, so attached to our identities as creatives with countless great ideas, read that title and rush to consume a heady tome on the act of creation we're so enamored with.

As with all things Seth, though, the punch line is stark.

His answer is simply this: "Decisions."

Also, as with all things Seth, he's right on the money.

But there's a catch here. If we business owners see our role simply as makers of decisions, then we do little more than poise ourselves at the receiving end of a batting cage with the mandate to swing all day long.

In order to preserve our creativity (and our sanity), then, we must learn to manage the decisions that lob themselves at us day after day. Otherwise, we won't have any energy left. Our prefrontal cortex will drop to its hands and knees panting, unable to make one more anything.

So right after her event, Charisse and I revisited her Decision Fatigue. Charisse's intention was to grow her events, both in size and number each year. To make this happen, she'd need to put the bulk of her energy toward her superpower, which was being the big, bright light in the center of the action. Not struggling with the tedious details of the event experience. Since Charisse discovered that those little decisions weren't going to make themselves as she disappeared into a Pringles can, she'd have to deal with them in a different way.

To get Charisse started, I shared something my friend and serial entre-preneur Dave Zumpano said to me early on as I was building my company and frustrated by a recurring problem with my team. Dave listened to me yammer on for a bit and then simply said, "Christine, where there's a stress, there's the lack of a standard." It was like someone handed me the combi-nation to a padlock I'd struggled with for years.

Charisse got it, too. "Ooo, that's a writer-downer!" she said. "So my stresses before the event are what'll show me how to do it better the next time?"

"Exactly," I said.

If we're not intentional, most of us will default to the typical approach to decision-making: reacting and wrestling the issue in the moment. After all, when you're starting out, it's just a decision here and a decision there. You can handle that.

But before you know it, this method becomes impossible. As your business grows, the balls keep coming your way, and you keep swinging. And as your brain gets tired, you may default to measures like whether or not you "feel" like it, which rarely turns out well.

The way to shift this pattern and preserve your brain is to think in terms of standards. By setting a standard and creating a system to support it, you eliminate the struggle of reacting all the time, of trying to figure everything out in the moment.

Setting standards comes down to two proactive practices:

1. Reducing the number of decisions you're faced with each day by making decisions in advance.
2. Creating general standards to guide your decision-making. So when the unexpected decision comes along, you have a structure in place to help you make it quickly.

These two practices get you out of the reactive mode and into the realm of creative decision-maker—making purposeful choices that align with your intention.

PRACTICE #1: MAKING DECISIONS IN ADVANCE

I didn't know what to wear, so I tore my closet apart, and now I'm late again!

I forgot to have breakfast. Now I'm starving and there's nothing but donuts!

I keep saying I want to write a book, but do I ever get around to it? No!

All these annoying people constantly interrupt my focus time!

If you've ever uttered a phrase like this—or more to the point, if you've uttered a phrase like this more than once—Dave would say you're lacking a "standard." You have a stressor screaming at you that could easily be eliminated with something I call a "decision in advance."

Want to have a solid breakfast before you start your day? *Decide in advance* by blocking out time on Sunday to plan, shop for, and assemble your breakfasts for the week.

Want to write your book? *Decide in advance* to devote an hour to writing it every day at 8 AM. Schedule it in your calendar, and let the world know you won't be reachable.

Want to stop tearing your closet apart each morning? *Decide in advance* by assembling a few standard "go-to" outfits.

When you decide in advance, you set the decision up at a time when you're not backed against the wall, rushing to figure things out. You do it intentionally, with focus. (And if you're new to this practice, you start small.)

When I shared this with Charisse, she said, "Oh! It's like Jennifer Aniston eating the exact same salad for lunch every day during the filming of *Friends*. She got to focus on her acting—and not worry about calories and macros."

"Sure," I said. "Or like Steve Jobs wearing his uniform black turtleneck every day. No need to waste brainpower on what to wear. You have much too important a role in the world to deal with that detail every morning. It's been decided in advance."

Examples of decisions in advance abound among all kinds of elite performers who need to ensure their focus remains in the right places. The trick is to treat yourself like an elite performer even if you don't feel like you warrant such treatment yet.

For that first event, Charisse's decisions had been the reactive kind, coming at her the minute they needed deciding. Which is understandable, being her first time and all. But now, planning for her second event, she was well aware of many of the decisions that would need making. So she and Alex set up a series of meetings to examine the stressors. And then to see which of those decisions could be made now—in advance. What could they streamline? Systematize? Or template? By making those decisions and creating structures for implementation, Charisse could confidently delegate the small stuff, allowing her to focus on the content and presentation.

PRACTICE #2: CREATING STANDARDS AND CRITERIA

When I was in my teens, I had a (very brief) job at one of those franchise cookie places at the mall. My assignment: to sell cookies. Lots of them. There were standards for how I was to do this.

Each time a customer came to the counter, I was to paste a smile on my face, "lift" my voice, and ask, "Would you like to buy six and get one free?" The store manager, appraising my performance from behind the swinging doors, would lean out and criticize me if I forgot to make the offer (which was often), or correct me if my inflection wasn't right (which was always), or insist I emulate the same level of enthusiasm as Angie, the ultra-perky blonde who worked the same shift (which was impossible).

I began to dread each customer's approach. When they smiled at me and pointed to the cookie of their choice, I would breathe deeply, swallow hard, and ask if they'd like to buy six and get one free. In my head, my thoughts would go, *No? You don't? Well, how about a pony then? Would you like to buy me a pony?!*

Needless to say, Angie, with her curling-iron curls and Bonne Bell Lip Smacker lips, kicked my ass up and down the cookie leaderboard.

When we hear about creating standards and criteria in our businesses, I suspect that at least some of us will resurrect some kind of mall job memory like this. The predictable lame scripts and robotic formulas dreamed up by guys in golf carts in Palm Springs all in an effort to keep the franchise alive with minimum-wage high school girls at the helm.

In these standards-gone-wrong scenarios, a valuable concept has been misused. (Or to paraphrase the iconic Ani DiFranco: "Every tool is a weapon if you hold it like a corporate drone.")

But standards, when you know how to create them and apply them, are an indispensable tool. They make things run better. Your clients and team come to rely on them. And you get to focus on building and creating instead of getting drained by daily interruptions.

Not every decision can be anticipated or made in advance. So, well-thought-out standards or criteria provide you with the guidelines and parameters for the ones that can't. This ensures your decision is congruent and on track with how you want things to work and the outcomes you expect.

Consider this real-life scenario, and adjust the details to fit your business.

You're going about your day when your assistant emails you. One of your clients is going to Greece for a month on vacation. He's decided he wants to double up his calls with you in the next three weeks, so he doesn't miss out on all the calls promised in the package you sold him.

Now, if you don't have many clients, you might get annoyed, but you could roll with this request and fit the extra calls into your schedule.

But if you have other clients, and you've already scheduled your time for writing, filming videos, having meetings, and spending time with your kids, this seemingly tiny request means sitting down and rearranging your entire schedule. It may also mean feeling irritated, even pissed off. (And perhaps guilty for the fact that you *feel* irritated and pissed off because you should be grateful to even have clients, right?)

Now you're facing a buffet of emotions on top of making a decision in the moment. Which probably means you won't make the most elegant of choices.

But what if you had set up standards already? What if your contract articulated this information clearly to your clients? And you've implemented an onboarding system whereby you've walked your clients through these standards? (If you have to miss a call, here's what happens. If you're ill, here's what happens.) With this in place, your assistant would just check in with you to let you know the request came in but that she took care of it by referring this client to his original contract and offered a solution based on those standards.

This decision is then made with very little impact on your emotions or your day. You've already done the hard thinking, setting the standards for requests like this. And you've protected your time, creativity, and confidence.

The most challenging part about setting up such standards and criteria is the aforementioned "hard thinking." And taking the time to do it. So a good place to start is to keep an ongoing list of current stressors. Then set aside time in your schedule to create a standard based on each stress for "how we do things here" in order to serve the client and you.

FOUR MAGIC WORDS TO COMMUNICATE STANDARDS

You'll notice that the above scenario requires that you, the leader of your business, can communicate standards cleanly and clearly. But most of us have never paused to think about our standards. Or to think about how those standards can serve other people and lead them, or even help us to do our work better. Instead, we constantly react. And we get snarky. "They have phones in Greece, right? And what with all this new technology out there, I'm betting you could even . . . wait for it . . . *Skype* me!"

Tempting as it may be to point out the obvious entitlement of this client, that's no longer your job in the world. You're not the teenager standing behind the counter at the cookie franchise. You're the owner of a business. You have clients who need you to act like said owner.

To that end, I teach my clients four magic words to use when communicating a standard: "Here's how this works."

For instance, let's say you set a standard to never have a sales conversation on the spot. And let's say someone is chomping at the bit at a cocktail party one evening and fires off the question you dislike most: "How much do you charge?" Instead of giving in to *their* agenda, you get to rely on *your standard*. You get to lead that person by saying: "Here's how this works." And then you go on to explain your standard of always scheduling time to talk on the phone about how you work. You share how this serves them rather than having a rushed conversation on the spot.

Or in the case of your Greece-bound client: "Here's how this works. As we discussed when we started working together, you and I have three sessions each month for the duration of your package. I set it up that way because it provides just the right amount of space between our work to give you time to implement and integrate. If you choose not to use those sessions as scheduled, you forfeit them. So it's totally your choice."

I call it "being in the alpha role." Setting standards puts you in the alpha role in your business—meaning *you* set the terms, not the client or the supplier or whomever. You tell the world: *Here are the parameters I've set for my operation.* And those standards create a protective foundation that keeps your business from falling prey to outside forces. When issues arise, you're not scrambling. You're not emotional. You look to your standards, and you know whatever decision you make will be aligned with your intention. This doesn't mean you never bend. But you don't bend automatically.

It is often said that we teach people how to treat us. I would add that through the standards you create, you teach everything how to treat you. "Here's how this works" places you firmly in the alpha role. Then, your standards guide the energies that move through your business, producing the outcome you desire.

But if you are not willing to set standards, you're teaching everything and everyone in your life to go ahead and do it their way and you'll adjust. You've defaulted to the socially acceptable mode of "being a nice person." This doesn't serve you, or anyone else for that matter.

IRRITATION IS A "STRESS," NOT A FLAW

There's a phenomenon that can happen to a business owner that causes all kinds of shame and guilt. It's a sudden or growing feeling of resentment toward a client, or maybe even all of your clients at once. The irritation and anger quickly turn into embarrassment at your pettiness. *When did I become such a bitch?*

More often than not, however, that resentment isn't evidence that you're a mean, horrible diva. Rather, it's an indication of a missing standard.

There's a scene in the '90s hit movie *You've Got Mail* where the Tom Hanks character says to Meg Ryan that it's business, not personal. Meg Ryan responds by asking what's so wrong with being personal anyway? She reasons, "Whatever else anything is, it ought to begin by being personal."

For the Soul-Sourced Entrepreneur, business is personal. How can it not be? Our business is an expression of us and our creativity. We put our heart and soul into this thing. So yeah, it's understandable that business is personal to us.

Often though, we confuse personal with "emotional." And those of us who land in a more sensitive place on the emotional spectrum feel like we personally can't function in a world that's all systems and standards. On the other hand, those of us who see the value of systems and standards regard emotions as the reason systems and standards break down. Whichever type you are, there's a lot of pushing, repressing, and judging when emotions enter a business.

There's no need to choose sides here. Emotions and standards can and should work hand in hand, if you let them.

The good thing about negative emotional responses is that they can show you where something is "off." In Dave's parlance: a stress. By now you know a stress is merely pointing to where a standard is needed. Once in place, these new standards return the favor to your emotions, giving you a process for resolving the irritation. Without that standard, all the natural stuff that comes up with clients can quickly turn into overwhelm.

So the next time you feel that irritation coming on, first explore if a set of standards and criteria might change the circumstances. If not, look at whether this is an ideal client. Finally, you can look to deeper issues you might be having. Usually, the irritation is nothing more than a stress, a red flag guiding you toward a standard, not toward a new round of medication.

YOU GETTING PAID: A DECISION IN ADVANCE

If it hasn't yet, the idea of paying yourself first will eventually find its way to your door. It sounds like a great standard. And it is. But if you're like many entrepreneurs, the idea hits you . . . then, a week or two later, so does the end of the month with only paltry rations in your bank account.

At this point, writing yourself a big fat check before paying invoices just seems wrong.

Of course it does. That's because this powerful standard—this decision in advance to "pay yourself first"—has now reverted to a reactive decision.

"Do I really pay myself when I owe other people?" Maybe you do. Maybe you don't. Or maybe you make some lame attempt and write yourself a check for twenty-three dollars because you love Michael Jordan.

But that, right there? That's the actual stress. That's what makes you wonder why so many people tell you this stupid one-liner with no realistic instructions for how to implement it. The truth is you didn't really make it *your* standard. You just adopted it as *a* standard, a good idea. Proof being that when it came right down to it, your bank balance—not you or your new standard—decided what you'd be paid this month.

That stress indicates that you need to invest a little more here. You need to gain some clarity on how to make this *your* standard, a standard you can commit to.

My client Holly found herself in that position.

Holly felt fearful about money. She only made $34,000 in her first year of business. But then, she jumped to $47,000. Though the trend was looking good, she was perpetually afraid that things might go south. And she made decisions in reaction to that fear. As a result, she never had enough money for herself.

Holly's partner Abby had a corporate job and would occasionally ask when Holly's business might bring in some regular cash for the household. "After all," she'd joke, "two black Labs aren't gonna feed themselves!"

Holly kept waiting until there was extra money each month. But after she paid the bills (her website alone required she make three payments), she never had any left over.

Then Holly heard me share my own story about paying myself first. Early on in my music career, I was still only making about $40,000 a year. Each month, I tried and tried to pay myself first but could never justify this new action, believing I was forever destined to be a starving artist.

But I decided to make the decision in advance. In my tiny office, I sat with my imaginary HR director, Maxine. I let her know that this business of mine had to start supporting "the talent." I officially requested that I make—for starters—$1,800 a month. I asked my accountant to help me set up the taxes and withdrawals. Then I was officially on my company's payroll.

You can view standards as a way to direct energy. "I'm in charge here.

And here's how I want this to flow." In the case of paying yourself, you're telling the money where you want it to go. It's like you're a gardener in an unpredictable climate. If you want to reap the harvest, you don't just sit back and pray for rain each year. You have to set up gutters and rain barrels to catch the rain, the energy. That way, instead of stressing out when it doesn't rain, you can now access that energy whenever you need it. You show that energy where you want it to go. "Hey, when you land on the roof, go into the gutters, and then down into the rain barrels."

In the case of paying yourself, you're doing the same thing with money.

When I set up my salary rain barrel, something was set in motion. Some might say that my decision made me more confident and relaxed in how I worked each day and let me stop feeling like I was getting the short end of the stick here in this business of mine.

Dave would say it eliminated the stress.

The metaphysical types would say I was telling the universe: "Okay, here's how this works from now on."

But my new standard, my decision in advance, worked. Within months, I noticed that I always got the performances and income I needed to cover my starter salary and pay the bills.

Holly was inspired by my story. But $1,800 was too scary for her. So she started with just $1,200. She created standards. She turned her bank account into a business account. She stopped paying any personal expenses from it. Then, she set up a direct deposit from her business account into her personal bank account. She even called it a "payroll," which sounded lofty at first. And she asked her accountant to help her with the taxes and deductions.

When she got her fifth new client only two months later, she began to wonder if there was something to this "decisions in advance" and "setting standards" thing. She felt proud. And she even bought the food for her two oversized, over-hungry dogs that month. The best part of all? The look on Abby's face when she high-fived Holly and said, "Wow! Look at you! A real paycheck!"

22

TOLERATING: THE ULTIMATE NON-DECISION

The late Stephen Covey, esteemed author, speaker, and productivity guru, famously warned that you don't want to climb the ladder of success only to reach the top and realize it's leaning against the wrong wall.

It's a cool metaphor. It's also a terrifying concept. One big, regrettable decision that lands you in a sudden and harsh reality. "Omigod, I'm a partner? I never even wanted to *be* a lawyer! I despise this whole profession!" Or, in your best David Byrne: "Well? How did I get here?" The stakes get mighty high when wrong walls are looming out there.

Consider this, though: Covey's oft-quoted metaphor ignores the very nature of ladder climbing, which involves movement. You know, steps. Over and over again, you'll be climbing that ladder, hoisting yourself up one rung at a time. Step A to step B may take years. Step A to step Z? A possible lifetime.

This means that if you were to continue to climb a ladder propped against the "wrong wall," those years would be filled with a relentless determination to ignore an assload of signs and signals all shouting to get off that particular ladder.

And this, my friends, is the real problem. Reaching the top of a wrong wall isn't a mistake made in a single moment (say, your decision to even *go* to law school).

No.

Your "wrong wall" means that you get midway through year one and notice you hate the classes, but refuse to pause and pay attention to your delight deficit. And you climb up one more rung.

Then you get to the end of year two and have to see a therapist to deal with your mounting depression. But you don't tell your fiancée because she's been working nights all in sacrifice to this brilliant life choice of yours. Another rung.

Finally, you finish law school, and the next rung is the clincher. You take a high-paying job in a city where you don't even want to live, all the while harboring a secret envy of your college roommate Jake, who started a food truck with a woman he met at Burning Man. Now they have a fleet of four trucks. And they're getting married next year right about the time you'll be digging out from snowdrifts before your morning commute to downtown Toronto.

You ignore all of it and just keep climbing.

Hold on, Christine, you might be thinking. *In this scenario of yours, I made the commitment to go to law school. Wrong wall or not, shouldn't I see that through? If we gave up on our dreams every time it got unpleasant or tough, where would we be?*

Well, maybe we'd be somewhere we actually wanted to be, or where we were truly meant to be, or at the very least, where we *enjoyed* being. If you'd paid attention to yourself on that law-school ladder—receiving and interpreting the incoming signals (your disinterest, your depression)—you may have realized that law stopped being your dream in that first year. Or that external forces (expectations and shoulds) were making your decisions for you and keeping you on that ladder.

Most importantly, you'd have noticed that somewhere along the way, you exited your initial energy of commitment and entered one of inertia. Otherwise known as "tolerating." And tolerating is the ultimate non-decision.

A GOOD IDEA AT THE TIME

At first, Brenda used air quotes whenever she talked about her business. She'd created a little "side hustle" (air quotes) with these cool "lifestyle and nutrition workshops" (air quotes). She'd been a dietician employed by hospital systems for so many years that it was hard to imagine this could become a "real business" (more air quotes).

Right from the start, Brenda's workshops created a buzz. Word spread until she was attracting more students and leading a regular series. She even added online components with a basic membership area. Eventually, she had to cut back her hours at the hospital because the "side hustle" (still with the air quotes) was making some real money.

At a hospital luncheon, Brenda ended up sitting next to Julie, a nurse. Julie had heard about Brenda's workshops and asked about them. Brenda mentioned that she needed to hire a virtual assistant. Julie, who'd been dreaming of cutting back her hospital hours, said, "Hey, I could totally do that!" And, bam, Brenda had her first "employee."

Having someone there to help her—even part-time—was heavenly. Brenda and Julie muddled through their first months together, laughing and bonding over the many challenges and mess-ups.

Brenda's business kept growing. She left her position at the hospital. And right about the time she stopped using air quotes, Julie stopped doing her job well.

The business's new systems and bigger list required a high level of skills with online platforms, email sequencing, and opt-in pages. Though Brenda paid for Julie to get extra training, emails were regularly going to the wrong people, auto-responders were failing to work, and students were landing on pages with "404" messages. At first, Brenda brushed it off, convinced Julie would get it eventually.

From the outside looking in, however, it was obvious. The job had outgrown Julie's skill set. And Julie wasn't making a move to change that. But to Brenda, it wasn't so cut-and-dry. She liked Julie. Julie had been there from the start. And hey, no one's perfect.

Another six months went by. Julie's work didn't improve. Brenda stopped bothering to have new ideas, knowing they couldn't be implemented. She worked weekends to keep up with the mounting issues. Then, because of Julie's inefficiency and outright blunders, the business lost money on a launch for the first time ever. This business that had once excited Brenda now felt like a grind. A low-grade anger was blistering under the surface.

TWO KINDS OF ENTREPRENEURIAL MISTAKES

At her first mastermind retreat, Brenda shared her situation with me. She asked if hiring Julie had been a mistake, admitting there were signs that Julie wasn't right from the start. She lamented that if she'd been smart and taken her business seriously, she would've hired someone with the right skill sets in the first place and saved herself a whole lot of heartache.

I asked Brenda to consider that she might be posing the wrong question in an attempt to dodge the real problem.

When Brenda hired Julie, it's true she acted without strategy or clarity. But it's also true she didn't really have both feet (or her head) in her business yet. She wasn't sure where this side hustle of hers was going and didn't know what would be needed. It was a fast decision. All perfectly normal and understandable. Now that she had more business experience, she could see the mistake she'd made by rushing.

In entrepreneur-speak, this is called a mistake of ambition. If you're going to make a mistake, this is a good one. You take a leap, and it doesn't work the way you thought it should. Your launch crashes; your idea loses money; the person you hired turns out to be a dud. To think you can get by in your business unscathed by mistakes of ambition and never smash face-first into some wrong wall is utter delusion. The most successful businesses pave the way with mistakes of ambition.

Even though Brenda's question was about this first kind of mistake, she was actually in danger of the second kind of mistake. I call it the mistake of toleration. That was the real culprit here, the true threat to her growing business.

Brenda's toleration of Julie and her inability to do the job had already cost the business its reputation with some clients. It had also cost Brenda frustration, time, and even her passion. Left to its own devices, Brenda's toleration was on track to undermine her business—or maybe even destroy it.

This mistake of toleration is where many business owners lose their way. That's because mistakes of toleration are hard to spot. They don't fall neatly into the category of "mistakes."

After all, mistakes *happen*. Tolerations accumulate.

Mistakes hurt. Tolerations annoy.

Mistakes can bring us to our knees and force us to find a solution, a better way. Tolerations let us create excuses: "What's all the fuss about? You should be happy to even have someone who wants to help."

It's easy to spot a mistake of ambition because you can pinpoint the exact instant you made the stupid decision—at that hospital luncheon when you didn't even attempt a formal interview or anything!

But mistakes of toleration are cumulative and punishing. You ignore the signs. ("That's strange, another client with the wrong access code.") You pretend you aren't frustrated. ("No, it's okay. Next week is fine.") You dismiss your needs. ("I'll just do it myself this weekend.") You may even criticize yourself for being too picky or demanding. Then you start bargaining with the situation. You even find "work-arounds" that make everything more complex, fixing other things, trying other methods, numbing and medicating yourself in a vain attempt to not deal with the real situation. (Brenda hired another virtual assistant to pick up Julie's slack, and suddenly her business was paying for two people to do the work of one. She also started drinking a second glass of wine with dinner.)

That's when you convince yourself—and everyone around you—that it's complicated. And while you may have indeed *made* it more complicated, it's actually not. It's just hard.

Here's why. All the fixes you make, the complexities you create, the excuses you sputter forth are games that help you avoid the one thing that's called for: facing the truth, and then acting on it.

ELIMINATING TOLERATIONS

An exercise I occasionally lead at our Uplevel retreats is to ask each person to list ten things they're tolerating in their business at that moment. Anything from the minor stuff (the sticky keypad on your laptop forcing you to retype the *M*, *N*, and *P* over and over) to stuff that makes us more nervous—the morning team meeting has lost energy, an employee keeps lying and I can see right through it, a client is crossing boundaries constantly.

The thing about tolerations, however, is that while a list can help you become aware of what you're tolerating, it doesn't help you with the harder part—the facing the truth and acting on it part.

Sure, the keyboard issue is a matter of taking it in for repair. It's unlikely you'll get much emotional pushback from the guy at the Genius Bar.

But restructure or change the morning meetings? Let someone go? Set boundaries with a client? The consequences can mean anything from days of pain to weeks of discomfort as you pay unemployment or deal with your team gossiping about the firing.

So how do we get up our nerve to act? To stop tolerating, own the truth, and start making decisions based on that truth?

Both parts of the process—recognizing our tolerations and putting an end to them—require trust. And not just any kind of trust. The hardest kind of trust to summon—trust in ourselves. In our needs. In our preferences. In our wisdom.

Once again, this calls for coming back to awareness and clarity around our intention. Then, trusting our interpretation so we're able to recognize when an employee, a situation, or even we ourselves are out of alignment with that intention. Then we draw energy from our commitment to that intention, trust in our wisdom, and make a decision that places us back in alignment.

It's not easy. It calls on us to overcome or at least manage some very primal fears. In some ways, toleration is in our DNA. No one wants to disrupt the status quo. To disappoint a client. To discipline an employee. To tell a supplier you no longer need their services. They might get mad at you. Or judge you. And you don't like that part. So your doubts stop you. Fear of being a jerk stops you. Fear of all the inconvenience stops you.

Through her work at the mastermind, Brenda was able to see what tolerating was costing her. She realized that the intention she initiated for her business wasn't about providing Julie with a paycheck. Her intention was about serving her clients. Julie's performance diminished Brenda's ability to do that. Giving more power to her fear of Julie's opinion of her than to her intention was hurting her business and her clients.

It would take many months for Brenda to actually let Julie go. As I said, this stuff isn't easy. But Brenda planned for the difficulty. She decided the exact day, scheduled a time, rehearsed the conversation she'd have with Julie, and asked her accountability buddy to be available to talk right after it happened.

There was drama. Julie "freaked out." She cried. She accused Brenda of being a terrible boss, a bad manager, and worse, a disloyal friend. Brenda stayed in her clarity and with her intention for her business. She didn't fight back. Brenda owned her decision. In her words, "I let her hate me. That was the worst part. I thought I would cave."

(Note here that Brenda didn't dump her newfound truth all over Julie. She didn't go into some long explanation about tolerations and how Julie had been bad for the business. That would've been unnecessary, cruel, and futile. Nobody needs to know your truth but you. Brenda stuck to the facts as rehearsed—the job had changed, new skill sets were needed, and though training had been offered, Julie showed little interest in acquiring those skills. The position was no longer the right fit.)

Within days, the pain lifted and Brenda was happy. Her other virtual assistant was happy. Her decision had liberated her. She was finally working with someone who had the right skill set. She understood the dangers in tolerating and was better able to see her specific patterns.

"Why did I wait so long?" she asked me, incredulous at her behavior. This is often the reaction we have when we break the pattern of tolerating. (No entrepreneur has ever said to me, "Wow. I should've waited longer before I fired that person.")

BUILT-IN EXCUSES

I used to perform at a summer concert series promoted by a woman named Jheri. Jheri was a DJ. She ran her own business, volunteered anytime someone with a cause needed volunteers, chaired on several boards, and also put this series together. Over the years, I'd gotten to know Jheri pretty well. But one summer when I showed up, she was pale and ragged. We were eating dinner before my show, and she shared some bad news with me. She'd been diagnosed with breast cancer.

As I listened to her talk about her next steps, she inserted a chilling comment. She leaned in and whispered, "You know what the best thing is about having cancer?" With a teenage-rebel grin, she said, "I finally have a built-in excuse to say no to all this stuff people want me to do, and they back off instantly." The smile remained but a shadow of defeat passed over her face. It took a deadly illness for Jheri to let herself own her preferences. To say no. To stop tolerating.

It's nice when we have a built-in excuse at the ready. "Be the keynote speaker at your first event for free? I'd love to but my little sister's getting married that weekend!" "Your high school son wants a summer job as my assistant? Oh, man, I just hired someone! Sorry!"

The real problem is that we think we *need* a built-in excuse. I celebrate when clients don't have built-in excuses. That's because not having that luxury forces you to own and express your truth and face the possible consequences, thus creating clarity and real strength. In the same way that "just tell me what to do" hands your power over to someone else, waiting for a built-in excuse lets you dodge your power by avoiding the discomfort of your clarity and preferences.

A steady habit of waiting for built-in excuses will ultimately land you at the place where you have no choice. In fact, rarely do our failures just *happen*, bam! You don't wake up one morning to discover you're eighty pounds overweight. (*Holy shit, how did that happen?*) A band of movers doesn't just show up at your door with a truckload of old furniture you don't want and ask you where in your house they should put it. And Brenda didn't just hire someone who was inept and say to herself, *Well, this here's a real head-scratcher.*

It doesn't work like that.

Each unmade decision, each moment you avoid your own clarity, each toleration piles up until your original intention is on a back burner somewhere. You run around doing everything but what you started your business to do. Until one day, you can't anymore. The business is in trouble. And you're so angry, so exhausted, and so off track, you think *you're* the problem. That you're just bad at business.

That's not it at all. What's happened here is that you've tolerated yourself into a corner. In addiction lingo, this is called "rock bottom." Just like addicts, tolerators get there by allowing the things we purport to care about—our intentions—to fall by the wayside in service to the very things that look innocent enough at first but in actuality undermine our dreams.

As long as we can keep up the front, we keep everyone loving us for not upsetting the applecart. Until one day, we wake up in that applecart in a back alley bloodied and bruised after a night of hard-core tolerating with no memory of how we got there. Then and only then do we say, "Oh man, something's wrong here."

If business is the playground for our soul's expansion, reckoning with tolerations is a full-blown discovery park—complete with bright, shiny objects to tempt you into doing what looks like the least trouble, mazes to confuse you as to what direction to take, and challenges to your trust in yourself. Toleration is always an option, enticing you to veer from your intention, avoid the painful decisions, and take the easy way out of any given situation.

For your business to be yours, you must make the decisions. You must trust yourself early on in a situation when you get that inkling that "this isn't working" or "something's not right." You must resist the temptation to paper over the problem with a toleration. And you must make decisions that align with your intention while you still have plenty of options.

You won't always do this well. You won't always be pure and free of transgressions or tolerations. But the more you tolerate in your business (and in your life) the more your energy is impacted by having to manage the incongruency between your intention and your actions. A willingness to navigate the uncomfortable territory of relentless clarity, trusting your intuition, and being honest with yourself is what creates freedom and true success for the Soul-Sourced Entrepreneur.

THE PIONEER AND THE ENGINEER

Tanglewylde Drive, Spartanburg, South Carolina, 1:10 PM

Jack Kinley, founder and CEO of The Collabo Group, was suddenly nine years old again. Or was it thirteen? Twenty-one? He could recall so many times when he'd wished his dad would actually see him, accept who he was, or just communicate with him without judgment, no matter how opposite they were. If his dad was the engineer—all science, math, contained and orderly—then Jack was the pioneer, all ideas, art, vision and disruption. For as long as he could remember, their conversations were relegated to judgments and dire predictions of Jack's demise if he didn't "straighten up."

Now, in Jack's fortieth year, in a single moment, a strange and delirious sensation surged through his whole being, as the words, "Jack, I want you to know that I'm so proud of you" hung in the air between them.

Admittedly, a snarky thought appeared. *It's the car.* On this visit, Jack had pulled into the driveway of his South Carolina childhood home in a high-tech BMW 5 Series he'd paid for with the success of the business he'd started just a few years before. Jack figured his dad saw the car as a sign that his son had finally become responsible. After all, this was slick machinery that would need to be looked after. The reality was Jack chose this car and got all the perks and services just so he didn't *have to* be responsible or waste time looking after anything, let alone a car. Inwardly, Jack rolled his eyes. *It's definitely the car.*

But his dad read his mind. "And it's not the car," he added

with a smile. "It's you. It's who you are. It's who you've become. You've done it *your* way. I'm so very deeply proud of you. I want you to hear that and know that."

Jack was speechless. His dad, who had only ever communicated any and all emotion through Jack's mom. His dad, who preferred to hide out in the basement with his ham radios, rather than hang out with the family. Who only ever emerged from that basement to express disappointment with his son—whether it was when Jack got his ear pierced, or forgot to change the oil on his first car and blew the engine, or the day he courageously drove from Atlanta to South Carolina to come out to his parents. Here was this stalwart man sharing his heart with his son, maybe for the first time ever.

That his dad had used the word "become" was significant, whether his father realized it or not. Jack's journey as an entrepreneur had been all about becoming. It started when he recognized he'd found his own brand of "hiding out in the basement," carrying on the pattern. He avoided decisions, and mostly just let things *happen*. In fact, the first time he made a list of things he tolerated in his life and business, it was almost two pages long. Each time he faced down one of those tolerations, he faced down a lifetime of avoiding his needs—a learned and applauded behavior in a Southern culture of quiet politeness.

Through an ongoing willingness to acknowledge such deep-seated patterns and manage them, Jack had become someone who got clear without getting resentful. He built a successful business from what really mattered to him: communication, acceptance, and diversity in company culture. He stopped using his many hobbies, ideas, and humor as distractions when things got tough with employees. He even allowed a bit of that engineer to inform his work habits.

Jack had stepped into the power of his decisions. He'd changed the name of his business from the more playful "Lab Monkey Design" to the intentional "Collabo Group." He'd married Cain, his life partner. He'd even bought the house they now loved and lived in. Everything had taught him to stay in the room, feel his own heart, and make clear choices.

Now his dad could see this, could see *him*. Clearly. And his dad was proud of what he saw. It would have been easy to make a joke to deflect the rawness and realness of the moment. But Jack stayed present, stayed in his body. He let the emotion course through him, and he did something he'd too rarely done in his life. He stepped forward, said, "I love you, Dad," and hugged his father.

23

GETTING GOOD AT DECISIONS

There you are. Being your passionate, idea-driven self.

And you meet someone. Maybe it's at a networking event. Maybe it's a friend of a client.

Either way, she finds out what you do. She lights up. And she says that she needs your exact services, only just a *little tiny bit different*, and could you possibly do this one other different thing for her, because, hey, she's heard good things about you?

And hell, who are you to turn down a little extra money in your business, right?

So even though the thing she wants is something you don't love doing, you create kind of a customized (and contorted) proposal just for this person. She's ecstatic.

So you, being you, hunker down and do the work.

Soon, someone hears about this thing you did, and says, "Hey, we were thinking about something just like that, only a *little tiny bit different*, like for a group setting and do you do group things like this?"

Well, as a matter of fact, you *don't* do group things like that. But, hell, you could learn right? That's how you've done everything, right?

So you—again, being you—make it up on the fly, don't sleep a whole lot, and ignore your other clients for a bit. But you pull it off and get paid.

Then another person comes along and says, "Wow. That's almost exactly what we need, *except for . . .*"

Pretty soon, you have a problem.

The problem isn't that you aren't smart enough to make these things happen. You are.

The problem isn't that you can't think on your feet and pull it off. You're doing just that.

The problem isn't even about the services themselves. Hey, you enjoy a few of them.

The problem is that these decisions you've made have nothing to do with your original intention. And now, you've *reacted* a business model for so long that you don't even remember what you wanted to create here. Or if you ever *had* an intention, not to mention what it was.

We entrepreneurs like to think we're Creative with a capital *C*. But when it comes to the practical reality of our day to day, the decisions we make are often *not* creative. They're Reactive with a capital *R*. Same letters. Different spelling. Radically different results, driven by a whole lot of unseen energy. The "unseen" part is the kicker: it means that realizing your intention requires having the courage to uncover what's behind the scenes, influencing your decisions. This is called self-awareness, and it's a key ingredient to making decisions that build a successful, congruent business that lights you up.

GETTING GOOD AT YOU

Let's revisit that Seth Godin "What do you make?" blog post. After alerting us that we mostly make decisions, Seth concludes by advising: "Make more decisions, that's the only way to get good at it."

But what does it mean to "get good at decisions"?

Most of us would say it means making the *right* decisions. And *right* decisions equal epic outcomes. Everlasting love. A book deal. Your first million. A new hire who takes your business to the next million after that. All with the added benefit of never failing or feeling anxiety again.

Sure, it's lovely when a decision leads to a great outcome. You get to pat yourself on the back and, for a few days or so, tell yourself the story that you've mastered the making of decisions. But this just turns decision-making into a sort of lottery. If you make enough decisions, maybe you'll find one that hits the happy-outcome jackpot. Then you can figure out how to get the world to stop so you can permanently gloat.

The reality is that, in any business, decisions lead to more decisions. So, as a Soul-Sourced Entrepreneur, consider that *getting good at decisions* really means *getting good at yourself* as the one who makes those decisions. That's much harder because it means getting good at seeing, with unflinching clarity, the many emotions and patterns—like fear, or shame, or revenge, or anger—that may be fueling your decisions. That can be tricky. And hard to navigate. Because these are subtle forces at work.

Maybe it looks like you said yes because it was an opportunity, which is what you tell yourself. But if you pause to take a gander under the hood, you discover you really said yes because you were scared to say no . . . because you barely made it through the last recession, which still haunts your every move. Or maybe you tell yourself you haven't raised your prices in five years because you want the masses to be able to afford your services. Underneath, however, it's your terror at being seen as an imposter that has driven your "nice girl" pricing philosophy. In fact, you've never even addressed how you set your prices. When left in the shadows, these emotions and patterns will run the show from behind the scenes with their own agenda.

Dr. Jill Bolte Taylor, neuroanatomist and author of the best-selling book *My Stroke of Insight,* describes her experience of lying in a hospital bed after a stroke at age thirty-seven. Though seemingly brain-dead, she fully experienced the energy and intention of each person who walked into her room. Her resulting directive to "please be responsible for the energy you bring to this space" has been quoted by many, including Oprah Winfrey, who hung those words on the outside of her dressing room. In other words, awareness of your emotional or mental state matters greatly. Same goes for the energy you bring to your decisions.

The nature of energy is that it doesn't go away. It simply moves into unseen crevices and spaces of your business. It morphs. And it attracts other similar energies—maybe fearful clients, and then fear-based tactics to deal with the fearful clients who now fill your business. Over time, you keep living into these decisions, often adapting further and further away from your intention and your truth.

SWITCHING DRIVERS

When Teri started working with me, she had a successful coaching business with a regular stream of long-term private and mastermind clients. She'd also recently started a membership site and was struggling to keep it going. With just seventy-four people paying a small monthly fee, Teri was constantly creating content for minimal financial return.

Another challenge was keeping the members engaged. She was used to serving a highly connected group of private clients, but the membership site was a totally different animal. The members weren't doing the work or showing up for the calls. They rarely connected and weren't motivated, and Teri didn't have the time or energy to be a cheerleader on top of everything else.

Her private clients (and her mastermind) were getting results. She lit up when she talked about them. Not surprisingly, this had been her original intention in her business.

I asked Teri to look back on her decision to start her membership site. What prompted such a radically different model when she already had clients and was doing pretty well?

"Um," she said. "I was scared."

Teri shared that a former client had gotten angry with her and went on an "unholy rampage." That client started calling and emailing Teri's other clients, making it her mission to put Teri out of business. Although the drama eventually died down, the experience had scared Teri so much that, in a quick knee-jerk moment, she chose to "pivot."

She decided to launch a membership site—*they were all the rage now*—thinking it would be a better option and hastily threw one together. She imagined that a large, somewhat anonymous group would keep her at a safe distance from the individual members, and any drama someone might create.

It's tempting to go right for the punch line here. Teri messed up. She bungled this thing big-time. But each and every one of us will do just this at certain points. We'll make decisions from fear (or any number of emotions that trigger us). The gift is being able to step back and take stock. Sometimes that's the only way to consciously recognize how a fear-based decision plays out in your world.

When fear drives our decisions, that fear energy carries over into our business to be lived out, often leaving us with a more chaotic circumstance and a more chaotic business. So when panic rattles you and you feel compelled to make a fast decision, pause instead. Get still and consider it might be a call to anchor back to your intention.

When I explained this to Teri, she balked. "I thought making decisions fast was the mark of a good entrepreneur! Like that Teddy Roosevelt quote? You know, 'In any moment of decision, the best thing you can do is the right thing, the next best thing is the wrong thing, and the worst thing you can do is nothing.' I didn't want to do nothing, you know?"

Now, I love good presidential wisdom just as much as the next guy. But the thing about quotes like this is we paste them into Evernote and then spout them off without considering all the context behind them. (Like perhaps Roosevelt had legions of smart people calculating the options and offering solutions—and that, when in battle with a gun to your head, you must indeed take action.)

To Teri, pausing and taking stock looked like the dreaded "nothing." And fear felt like all the "something" she needed to force a decision, using a handy quote to justify her avoidance of the real issue. (More context: Roosevelt was known for long periods of silence and contemplation.)

Teri and I backed up and looked at her membership numbers, at the revenue, at what each income stream meant to her, and at how much time and energy each required. We considered what it would take to really build the membership—and she explored whether she actually wanted to do that. It was an option, for sure. But when she got clear, she knew it wasn't what she wanted her business to be or to provide. She valued connection, coaching, and working with people one-on-one. And she was good at it. So with that in mind, she made a different decision, anchoring back to her intention.

It took a few months to find the way and the courage, but Teri carried out her new decision. In spite of her fears (abject poverty and people disliking her), she composed the emails, shutting down the membership site, telling the truth, and offering other options for coaching. A few people were irritated. Many responded with understanding. Several joined her mastermind. A few signed up for private coaching. Most important, Teri was back on track, doing the work she loved, the work she intended, and her business became manageable again.

WHAT COURAGE LOOKS LIKE

Scroll through your Instagram feed on any given morning, and you'll find reams of motivational messages about courage, paired with images of mountaintops, tough mudders, kettlebells, and big heroic leaps.

What you won't find in those messages is an image of a lone business owner at their desk having a mild panic attack as they're about to hit send on a sensitive email that—for the first time in that person's life—sets a boundary. Or someone ripping another cuticle off with her teeth as she makes a decision to close down her membership site, while being rocked by a committee of critical voices in her head.

Getting good at decisions is the ultimate courage and the ultimate trust. It is brave to face down an old pattern that's been driving you. It is brave to make a decision that lands you in uncertain territory.

Getting good at decisions has nothing to do with perfect outcomes. Decisions are more a practice than a done deal. They're fluid, not fixed. That's the good news. Every decision—even a reactive one—holds the potential to expand and advance you, if you're open to discovery. A decision made from a place of fear, for instance, may produce a situation that lays your fear bare (like it did for Teri). If you can call in your awareness, that decision is now providing the opportunity to explore that fear, deal with it, and create a new, fear-free decision anchored in your intention. Business is territory for your soul's growth, after all. And nowhere is that more evident than in your decisions.

24

REAL IS THE NEW STRONG: EMBRACING YOUR FUNK

The first time I saw the automotive product Rain-X in action, I was a passenger in a car that was forging through a downpour. It was dark, we were lost, and we were hopelessly late for our dinner reservation. I wasn't worrying about directions or parking spaces, though. I chose instead to marvel at how the rain literally seemed to avoid the windshield. That's when my date explained that he'd coated it with Rain-X that morning. I felt like a college stoner staring at my roommate's lava lamp: "Whoa. Duuuuuude. What *is* that?"

Later that week, at lunch with some friends, I shared my Rain-X discovery. As my friend Brian stuffed his Reuben into his mouth, he said, "When they make one for humans called Asshole-X, I'll be the first to bathe in it." His wife Rachel added, "Or Takes-It-Personally-X." We then came up with the many names for a product that could coat us in a thin veneer and repel the stuff we'd rather not deal with. Invincibility is compelling.

But invincibility is not about protective coatings. If there is such a thing as being invincible, it has a lot more to do with a deep trust of what's inside you than it does with shielding yourself from what's outside you. The true and unlikely source of our strength is our realness, our authenticity. And as we've discussed throughout this book, that includes emotions, weaknesses, sensitivities, traumas, triggers, and triumphs. Being able to use everything we are as the raw material for expansion and growth is what keeps that expansion and growth fresh and real. This makes your work dynamic, and it creates the discovery and the upward trajectory that are so coveted in business.

When you work with the principles in this book—intention, power, interpretation, decision—you let your business and life guide you and show you how to take action and how to break through the unconscious things that have become shields likely holding you back, even as you pretend they're protecting you.

Josh Waitzkin, chess prodigy turned martial arts champion and occasional reluctant guest on the Tim Ferriss podcast, teaches an idea called "embracing your funk." This means the very things you might consider weaknesses, quirks, and oddities are the exact things that—when accepted, infused, and embodied—become the core elements of your high performance. Most of us are so focused on fixing (or, at the very least, hiding) these vulnerable parts of ourselves that we have no clue how *embracing them* could possibly work. That idea represents a total paradigm shift. It's a paradigm shift that my clients have experienced and celebrated over and over again, remarking that while the resulting financial rewards are indeed wonderful, the biggest reward is who they've become in the process: entrepreneurs and creatives who are strong, clear, unafraid of their power, and able to move through the many events in their business without shielding themselves with the usual defense tactics.

The real success in any business is the freedom to navigate the terrain in your natural state, not having to spend each and every day controlling anything that threatens to make you uncomfortable or faking some phony mindset so people won't judge you. I once heard Buddhist teacher and author Tara Brach use the phrase "impression management" to describe this manipulative approach. It's an attempt to control the outside, or other people, or circumstances. And it's exhausting and debilitating. Thankfully, as we now know, there is another way.

While playing with several possible subtitles for this book, I was struck by the number of people who recoiled at the word "sensitive." Some said it was inappropriate for a business book. Others said it would turn people off.

At some level, this is understandable. We've all been in those relationships with "sensitive" types who somehow manage to pair "sensitive" with "broken," demanding special handling, often accompanied by accusations and entitlement. But that's just an attempt to create a shield. If we adhere to a strict definition of "sensitive," then it's about being keenly aware. Or to quote the dictionary on my MacBook: "quick to detect or respond to slight changes, signals, or influences."

If you started and now own and run a business, then you clearly have this quality, this "funk" Waitzkin speaks of, whether you see it as a strength or a liability. I have somehow made a niche coaching people on how to start, market, and run their businesses while being exactly who they are. I've had the honor of working with some of them for four, five, six, even eight years. The change in their whole being is staggering. They walk into the room at our retreats, and their energy is entirely different from their first days in that same room. They're able to embrace who they are, lose the protective stance, and embody a success that is assured, calm, confident, and peaceful.

I so wish it were an overnight process, but it's not. It does, however, begin with two simple words: "I'm In." At a time when noise, drama, and blatant reactionary aggression is the norm, your choice to say these words and then live into them is nothing short of a revolution for you and the people who are impacted by you in this important work you do. Here's to embracing your funk and joining the transformative world of the Soul-Sourced Entrepreneur.

ACKNOWLEDGMENTS

From the day I started hosting small retreats to the year I stepped into the full-time role of coach, I've had the honor of working with so many wildly beautiful souls. My clients (my "peeps") are the heart of this book. Your intention, courage, vulnerability, and even your pushback have shaped not just the content on these pages, but that of my life as well. Thank you for trusting me to guide you.

To my agent Scott Hoffman at Folio Literary Management, thank you for truly "getting" this odd little book you received after a chance encounter by a bank of empty coffee dispensers. Also, for your encouragement not to self-publish and pushing me so hard on my writing, not to mention your expert wine lessons at Ten Bells! And to Jan Baumer at Folio for being my go-to BFF agent and sounding board. Your vast experience, insight, laughter, and empathy have been indispensable.

At a time when authors are told they can whip out entire books in ninety minutes and become self-published superstars in weeks, I felt like a Luddite when I decided to go old-school and write (like, for reals) this thing that became my first book. In the process, I've discovered it takes innumerable brilliant people for a book to find its way out into the world.

Mary Carol Moore, you coached me when I had nary a clue how one might take reams of chaos and turn it into an organized framework.

Without your initial belief, teaching, editing, and coaxing, I wouldn't have started.

Beth Brand, this book wouldn't exist without you. You brought order, equanimity, encouragement, and love to it. Thank you for being my catcher's mitt, organizer, editor, and ninja writer-in-my-pocket. (And for all of your "LOLs.") You are a treasure.

Thank you to the brilliant team at BenBella. Glenn Yeffeth, for believing in this book and being so present and ready to talk, think, and ideate together. Also to Alexa Stevenson, Sarah Avinger, and Scott Calamar for the extreme patience, care, and skill you bring to the table. And of course, Greg Brown: I can't imagine working with a more perfect editor, fellow musician, and future best-selling novelist. Your keen eye, writing skills, and commitment made it fun.

To Jack Kinley, for designing such a gorgeous cover worthy of any Glitter Pony. (And to Cain, for prodding Jack. And Clyde, just cuz.)

Let it be known that working for a Soul-Sourced Entrepreneur is a full contact sport. The people on Team Uplevel are the ones who keep it all running and keep this 10 Quickstart from crashing into walls. A million thank-yous for the skill sets and commitment of Silvia Saunders, Renee Clements, Erin Louis, Adam Carlan, Erin Tillotson, Kinsay Sand, Jackie Stone, and Gary Henderson. Finally, Amanda Evans, I don't even know how many years it's been, but with each passing day, I'm evermore grateful for your commitment, follow through, focus, and tirelessness. (And your funny voices.) It's no wonder our clients say, "I want my own Amanda!" A special hat tip to Andrew Zetterholm for your grounded perspective, relentless commitment, and integrity for seven years.

Through Uplevel's ten years, I've been blessed to work with a team of coaches, each one a Soul-Sourced Entrepreneur in her own rite. Their passion, expertise, and attention have upleveled the entire program. Thank you to Sara Arey, Robbin Jorgensen, Whitney Bishop, Robin Barr, Christine Springer, Kelly Ruta, Jen Roberts, Colleen O'Grady, Sara Dickison Taylor, and Jenn Flynn. And last but definitely not least, Elaine Bailey Anderson . . . who left not only her business, but also her country, to lead this coaching team. Elaine, your unflinching belief and expertise have been a force field of strength. Thank you for taking on the all-too-complex role of colleague, coach, friend, and employee. I'm so grateful for your presence in my life. (ME TOO!)

This book wouldn't exist without those clients who let me share their true stories and use their real names and businesses. A million thank-yous to Sue Ludwig (moo), Robbin Jorgensen, Michelle Knox, Carolyn Connell, Triana (a.k.a. Tisha) Cordoza, Connie Sobzcak, Ginger Meek Allen, Carrie Frye, and Jack Kinley.

Thank you to the whole "Kane Fam" for love, encouragement, and always being there: Mom (for listening to early excerpts and always raving), Paula, Stephen, Brian, and Olivia. I love you more than words can say!

And to my dearest friends who listen and love without fail: Kathy LaMotte, Francesca Huffman, Joy Letsinger, Bob Damiani, Phil Weast, Keith Bramlett, Susan Piver, Sue Ludwig (moo again, this time with a Chuck Jones cartoon), Lisa Larter, Karen Smith, and Brooke Castillo.

And to Pamela Bruner who listened to me ramble on at length and simply said, "I'm In!"

The best mentors and coaches are those who live what they teach. I've been blessed by the guidance of many stellar mentors. Most especially I want to thank those who directly influenced the content of this book: Thom Politico, Dan Sullivan, Randy Nelson, Angela Ditch, Barb Da Costa, Hiro Boga, Dave Zumpano, Bari Baumgardner, and Lissa Friedman.

Lastly, I am deeply grateful to Mickey Gamble, my cheerleader, confidante, and Yoda through music, entrepreneurship, strategy and soul. ILYVM.

ABOUT THE AUTHOR

Photo by Kristi Hedberg

CHRISTINE KANE is the founder of Uplevel You, a multimillion-dollar business-coaching company, which was a natural evolution from her fifteen-year career as a touring singer-songwriter with her own record label. Both businesses were built from scratch without a single investor. Learning as she went, she did it all step-by-step and now shares this wisdom with her clients, so they finally get it, apply it, and succeed on their own terms. Her company's masterminds, trainings, and events draw entrepreneurs from around the world. She lives in Asheville, NC, where she hikes, hugs trees, rescues too many cats and dogs, and has a back squat best of 210 pounds.